Praise for Bread and Chocolate
by Fran Gage

"Reading this collection of Fran Gage's short food fables h
settling in a comfortable chair next to her, delving into her
and memories. Meeting Fran through her words and recipes is like tasting one of her plum tartlettes. Her recipes burst off the pages with zesty flavor. Her stories offer a rich, deep sense of the textures of food and of life itself. This is a book to keep bedside and in the kitchen!"

—Antonia Allegra

"Fran Gage's charming book of food essays is as irresistible as a warm croissant. Her enviable adventures in food-focused Northern California will remind many of us why we live there."

—Janet Fletcher, *San Francisco Chronicle*

"Fran Gage's prose is as delicious as her recipes. *Bread and Chocolate* ranks with the best food writing of the 20th century."

—Nick Malgieri, author of *How to Bake*

"In *Bread and Chocolate,* Fran Gage has captured how important food, friends, and good eating make our lives enriched and fulfilled."

—Chef Roland Passot, La Folie

"With personal stories, this book lovingly captures the diversity of San Francisco Bay Area food stuffs and the folks who produce them. Although a baker, Fran's recipes go way beyond 'bread and chocolate.'"

—Bruce Aidells, co-author of *The Complete Meat Cookbook*

BREAD AND CHOCOLATE

BREAD AND CHOCOLATE

MY FOOD LIFE IN & AROUND SAN FRANCISCO

Best Wishes FRAN GAGE *Fran Gage*

SASQUATCH BOOKS
SEATTLE

Printed in the United States of America
Distributed in Canada by Raincoast Books, Ltd.
03 02 01 00 99   5 4 3 2 1

Cover and interior illustrations: Cyclone Design
Book design: Karen Schober
Composition: Kate Basart
Copy editor: Rebecca Pepper

Library of Congress Cataloging in Publication Data
Gage, Fran.
    Bread and chocolate : my food life in and around San Francisco / Fran Gage.
        p.   cm.
    Includes index.
    ISBN 1-57061-153-X
    1. Bakers and bakeries—California—San Francisco. 2. Cookery. 3. Pastry. 4. Cookery
(Chocolate). I. Title.
TX763.G25   1999
641.8'15—dc21   98-49610

Sasquatch Books
615 Second Avenue
Seattle, Washington 98104
(206) 467-4300
www.SasquatchBooks.com
books@SasquatchBooks.com

Sasquatch Books publishes high-quality adult nonfiction and children's books related
to the Northwest (Alaska to California). For more information about Sasquatch Books titles,
contact us at the address above, or view our site on the World Wide Web.

For Neen

CONTENTS

Recipe Contents

ACKNOWLEDGMENTS

I HAVE RECEIVED THE SUPPORT OF many people as I wrote these words and would like to thank all of them. Some of that support began long before I ever intended to write a book. Flo Braker had encouraged me for years to consider a book project. The first time she made the suggestion, I looked at her in disbelief. That didn't stop her; her encouragement continued and I thank her for her persistence.

My bakery, and consequently this book, would never have existed without the hard work of the staff, who kept things running and helped me realize my vision. Nor could the bakery have continued without the loyal customers who returned again and again.

Jeannette Ferrary and Jane Anne Staw, and the members of their classes, helped me translate loosely structured thoughts into sentences and then into paragraphs.

A stalwart group of recipe testers, Sandy Mullin, Marion Norberg, Jennifer and Les Seely, Bernadette Kramer, Phyllis Baldenhofer, Ed Dunlap, and Kathleen Murphy, pointed out confusions and inconsistencies.

Paula Linton was always ready with an obscure piece of information, Ann Martin gave me valuable Internet addresses, and the staff of the special collections room of the library at the University of California at Santa Cruz went out of their way to send me documents. Georgia Peter, Phil Fendyan, Carolyn Harrison, Bart Minor, and Larry Stickney also shared experiences and answered questions.

Martha Casselman has been continuously supportive and encouraging. I thank her for finding Gary Luke at Sasquatch, and I thank him for trusting that I could write these pages.

All of the people mentioned in this book—the farmers, harvesters, and makers of good food—were very generous, talking to me and inviting me to visit their farms, plants, and boats. I also thank Ig Vella, Kathleen Weber, Michael Recchiuti, Kathleen Stewart, and Lindsey Shere for generously spending time with me.

Food-loving friends have shared countless meals and culinary adventures with my husband and me. These hours have let us enjoy an important pleasure of life and have brought us closer together.

My children, Casey and Claire, who grew up during the years that the bakery was a dominant theme in our family and eating dinner together was an important part of our lives, took it all in and crafted their own definition of what constitutes good food.

My deepest gratitude is to my husband, Sidney, who read every word and ate every dish. More importantly, he was the one who really started it all when he suggested that I write an account of a trip to France for the bakery's newsletter.

BREAD AND CHOCOLATE—
AN INTRODUCTION

I HAD A BAKERY IN SAN FRANCISCO. The Fran Gage Pâtisserie Française sat at the top of Eighteenth Street, a block below the final curve in Market Street just before it straightens out and heads downtown. When upper Market Street was built in about 1917, part of the building was lopped off, changing its shape from a rectangle to a wedge. A photograph from that year shows that it was a bakery then, Danvers Bakery, and it was for sale. I don't know what became of it.

I opened my bakery in 1984 and closed it in 1995 following a fire. Although I had been running a wholesale baking business from my house, I had never worked in a commercial kitchen. But this didn't dampen my enthusiasm. When the opportunity arose, I rented the former Danvers Bakery and installed a French-style pâtisserie. The move liberated our home from fifty-pound sacks of flour, thirty-pound boxes of nuts, and employees arriving before dawn. It was an odd setting for a retail store, six blocks up a steep grade from the neighborhood's commercial district. But it was the perfect place for me. I lived down the street with my husband and two young children.

The store opened at the beginning of December. I thought we had made an impossible quantity of *bûches de Noël* that first Christmas, but I was wrong. Each year this number of orders increased, and we worked at a furious pace to fill every one. A friend soon wanted bread for his charcuterie, so we made a few loaves for our store as well. Little did I know that we were at the forefront of a budding artisanal bread movement. People were hungry for handcrafted bread with a flavor developed by long fermentation times. The bread business grew dramatically. Soon we were delivering bread as well as pastry to other retail stores and restaurants.

To accommodate all the baking in a thousand square feet, I eventually moved the bread production to the night. There were only a few hours, just before dawn, when the bakery was empty.

As the business evolved, I continued to learn. During the second year, I went to France for a bread-making course to augment my self-taught skills. A few years later, an interest in pulled sugar (fancy sugar decorations) sent me back. In 1989, I returned for a chocolate course. This knowledge spurred a line of chocolates that were added to the bakery's other offerings.

Word spread about my bakery. People traveled across the city for *croissants,* whole wheat bread with walnuts, raspberry tarts, and made-to-order birthday cakes. Two years after we opened, Gerald Asher, the wine editor for *Gourmet,* wrote an article about shopping in San Francisco for the magazine, and included my store. He arrived one day in a limousine accompanied by two editors and a photographer. My bakery was in a national publication. He returned some years later when he was driving his friend Elizabeth David around to Bay Area food spots. At first he entered the bakery alone to buy bread, explaining that Elizabeth wasn't feeling well and had opted to wait in the car. After leaving, though, he didn't drive away. Moments passed. Then he got out of the car again, opened the passenger door, and helped his friend make the short walk to our front door. My staff pushed me to the counter. "Go talk to her, Fran." But I was speechless. Two legendary food writers were standing in my small bakery. Elizabeth David said some wonderfully complimentary things about what we made, then they left again.

We were frequently cited in the local food media. In 1992, *Bay Food,* a local paper, held its second International Bread Competition. Local bakeries were invited to participate; the Ritz-Carlton hotel hosted a reception; and French, Swiss, and German loaves were air-freighted overnight. A panel of local food experts judged the offerings. When, with great fanfare, the winners were announced, our *pain au levain*, a sourdough bread made without commercial yeast, had won first prize in its category. I had always thought it was our best bread and was proud and excited that others thought so too.

My childhood years didn't foreshadow these developments. We ate home-cooked Irish food—potatoes every night accompanied by meat, except on Fridays when we had fish. The only baking I did was making Christmas cookies every year. When I was a teenager, my father took up pie making. He developed a crust using vegetable oil and filled the pies with fresh fruit when it was available and canned when it was not. He was very proud of his pies. They were tasty, especially the fresh apple.

My final semester of college gave me a taste of the reality of cooking every day. Six of us negotiated our way out of the horrors of dining hall food. We were nursing students, working off campus in hospitals all day. Therefore, we reasoned, we should be allowed to use the tiny kitchen off the foyer in the dorm to cook our meals. The powers that be accepted the plan. We ate quick breakfasts standing in the kitchen before the dining hall was open, while two people made sandwiches to take for lunch. In the evening, we took turns cooking, then ate at a table in the lounge. Friends joined us ("Hey, look what the nurses are cooking tonight!"); there were often ten for dinner. Spaghetti with a canned tomato sauce and maybe a green salad were frequent offerings.

A year after we married, Sidney and I took our first trip to Europe and crisscrossed our way through France by motorcycle. That trip changed the way I thought about food. Although my family ate dinner together when I was growing up, the food was secondary. In France, what was on the table assumed a presence of its own. It was there for enjoyment as well as nourishment; the pleasure of eating was linked to the friendship of gathering at the table. Sometimes the food can rise above the table onto a pedestal, becoming as intrusive as flickering candles at eye level. But this didn't happen in the modest restaurants where we ate, usually small dining rooms in the countryside where groups of friends or families shared meals. Once, after a long drive to an out-of-the-way inn, we arrived only to find it closed. Seeing our disappointment, the proprietor agreed to take us in and feed us, as he was already at the stove preparing food for friends who had been hunting. The hunters, still in their outdoor clothes, assuaged their appetites with several courses and bottles of wine. The setting let them recount the adventure of the day, enjoying it again. From across the room, Sidney and I vicariously shared their pleasure.

That trip inspired me to expand my cooking skills. I worked my way through Julia Child's books, tackling dishes we had tasted in France, attempting things we had never eaten. As my repertoire expanded, more culinary doors opened. Sidney and I often cooked together, organizing the order of battle and bantering about details. One year we made cassoulet for a Christmas party. The next year we repeated the menu, inviting more people. The final year of the party, we crammed fifty people into our four-room Victorian flat, baking the cassoulet in a complicated tiered system in our old O'Keefe & Merritt oven. Sharing our culinary adventures with friends made creating them even more enjoyable.

Five years after our awakening trip to France, we returned to Europe for a three-year stay. Sidney had persuaded his employer to transfer him, not to Paris, our hoped-for destination, but to Brussels. The move opened another culinary chapter in our lives. We ate hearty Belgian fare: *frites, moules, waterzooi.* I shopped for food on our neighborhood market street, making my way from the store where a quiet man sold pristine fruits and vegetables that customers weren't permitted to touch to the poultry and game store with feathered pheasant, wild boar, and *canard de Barbarie.* One year, I ordered a goose for Christmas from this store. The proprietor waved his arm at a group of birds hanging by their necks and asked me which one I wanted. Not noticing any differences, I pointed to one, then for one horrifying moment thought he was going to wrap it up on the spot, plumage and innards intact. When I asked him if the bird could be cleaned, he looked insulted. *"Mais oui, Madame. Vous revenez demain."* I returned the next day to retrieve my prize. A few doors away, a bakery made marrons glacés. A block from our apartment, a woman had a small cheese store with an impeccable selection. Across the street from her shop, a fish store sold oysters from the coast. I bought things I had only read about, then rushed home and combed cookbooks for recipes.

A bustling market filled the square in front of the south train station each Sunday morning. Its stalls sported odd kitchen gadgets, clothing, vegetables, plants, and an array of herbs and spices, many unfamiliar, used by the city's Arabic populace. Sidney's favorite stall was the grill, where he always bought a blood sausage on a piece of baguette, dripping with grilled onions. It didn't seem like breakfast food to me.

There was another outdoor market on the outskirts of the city that I traveled to on the tram. I bought mussels enclosed in mesh bags, Bintje potatoes, tiny green beans, and kilos of whatever else was in season, lugging them from the tram stop to our home two blocks away. One cold Friday afternoon, a van stopped in front of our living room window. The driver rang a bell, got out, and opened the side of his truck. I thought I recognized him from the market. He was the fishmonger, returning to the coast, stopping in a few neighborhoods to sell the last of his fish, still glistening on the ice. I bought a Dover sole that day, at a good price. On subsequent Fridays, I watched for him and hurried to his van to select other wonderful fish from the Atlantic, many superior, I think, to those pulled from Pacific waters.

Belgians love to eat, and there were many restaurants to try. We frequented them as often as our budget allowed—the prices were shocking. A young up-and-coming chef ran one of our favorites. I drove to his restaurant the morning following a particularly satisfying meal and, in faltering French, asked if I could watch him cook. He graciously invited me to come as often as I wanted. Although I offered to chop parsley, peel potatoes, do anything, he always declined. So I took notes instead. The only other woman in the kitchen was the dishwasher. Today, his restaurant, Bruneau, holds three stars from the *Guide Michelin*.

The recently opened La Varenne cooking school lured me to Paris, where I spent two sweltering weeks in July expanding my knowledge. Later, the Parisian restaurants lured Sidney and me as well. It was an exciting time. The critics, Gault and Millau, were ferreting out chefs cooking with a lighter hand, challenging the *Michelin* decisions, so there were many choices. Trips to Paris, with our good friends who had moved to Holland from San Francisco, became carefully planned visits. A highlight was our New Year's dinner at Taillevent in 1976. I can still almost taste the goodness of that evening—small molds of chicken liver mousse, pink inside, with a thick tomato *coulis* on the plate; a delicate seafood sausage, studded with truffles and pistachios, bathed in *beurre blanc*; a squab, cooked in a copper pot sealed with dough, like a *daube*, served in the pot with a sauce of truffles and quickly sautéed pieces of liver; and a *gateau aux trois parfums*—chocolate, mint, and pistachio. At midnight, the kitchen staff appeared, striking copper pots with wooden spoons in a dignified manner befitting the atmosphere.

We didn't confine ourselves to Paris. A pilgrimage to Burgundy to buy wine became an annual fall event. During one of those trips, we took turns walking and soothing our fretful six-week-old son Casey in the *cave* of a Côte d'Or wine merchant. At eight months, Casey traveled with us again for our gastronomic pilgrimage to favorite places before we moved home to San Francisco. Back in Burgundy on that trip, at the restaurant Lameloise in Chagny, we asked if a meal could be sent to our room for him. A covered plate of poached fish, steamed potatoes, and *haricots fins* arrived. He ate it all—his first meal in a three-star restaurant.

When we returned home, I couldn't find some of the things we had grown to love, including *haricots fins*. Arugula was an unknown salad green, and sorrel and chervil didn't exist. I ordered seeds from an obscure company and planted my own. Now the greens, some organically grown, are available in supermarkets, and tiny green beans are plentiful at farmers' markets.

Our reentry was before the plethora of farmers' markets that abound today, although there were farms that welcomed visitors and let people pick their own fruits and vegetables. I organized a day trip for Sidney and our two young children (Claire was born in 1979), thinking that the kids would enjoy being farmer for a day. Picking raspberries in the hot sun bored them in fifteen minutes. I was the only one who had fun.

My specific interest in baking developed after we had been home for a few years. The process fascinated me. It was different from cooking—more exacting, a different sort of chemistry. At home with two young children, I started making bread, using recipes from Bernard Clayton's *The*

Breads of France, trying to re-create the loaves we had eaten in Europe. Then my thoughts turned to French pastry. There were challenges to be met: thin sheets of *biscuit*, unctuous buttercream, rich chocolate fillings and coatings, cakes with finishes as smooth as glass, complex textures and tastes in one bite. I found out about a school near Paris run by the famous pastry chef Gaston Lenôtre where I could find the answers I sought. I packed my bags and soon, flanked by serious students from around the world, was hard at work unraveling pastry mysteries. The time at the school redirected my life. I became consumed by French baking.

In this book I offer stories about food adventures and recipes inspired by them. Many spring from the bakery; others were developed with fellow food enthusiasts. There are underlying currents—a curiosity for more knowledge, a nostalgia for specific memories, the excitement of a new discovery, an appreciation of the bounty of Northern California, and most of all, an understanding of the way that food draws people together and deepens their friendship.

Tomatoes of my Childhood

I can't remember the taste of the Mrs. Paul's Frozen Fish Sticks that I often ate for Friday night dinners during my Catholic girlhood in Pennsylvania, but I do remember the taste of the tomatoes from my father's backyard plants. Chosen for their perfectly ripe state and picked just before dinner, they were still warm from the summer sun. A washing under the cold tap removed the garden dirt and cooled the fruit. Usually they were sliced and placed atop a bed of iceberg lettuce and doused with a bottled dressing. Those tomatoes were red the whole way through, meaty, juicy, and sweet. We ate them every day during the summer. Sometimes for a snack I would pick one or two in the garden, dispense with the washing, and just stand there among the plants, eating them like apples.

Three or four tomato plants are generally enough for a family of four, but for some reason my father would plant about three dozen. In late spring he headed out to the garden wearing a sleeveless undershirt and a pair of old pants. He turned over the dirt behind the back lawn with a pitchfork, then raked it smooth. After the plants went into the ground, he positioned a wooden stake next to each one. As the plants grew, he secured them to the stakes for support, using strips of rags from the basement.

The plants produced far more than we could eat, so my mother would "put them up" in marathon canning sessions, usually during the hottest and most humid days of the summer. I was enlisted to cut off stems and blanch off skins in huge kettles of boiling water. She canned some as they were and added onions and bell peppers to others. The packed quart jars were stored in the basement along the wall farthest from the coal furnace, where they stayed cool. During the winter she used the tomatoes in stuffed peppers and poured them over meat loaf.

I think that my father bought plants, not seeds, for his garden, and I don't know what variety of tomato they were—probably one of the old varieties, called "heirloom" tomatoes today. Since the days of my father's garden, hybrid tomatoes have come into vogue, being disease resistant, mildew resistant, hardier, and more productive. In 1994, hybrids were taken a step further, to genetically engineered species—perfect red spheres whose taste bears no resemblance to the tomatoes of my childhood. I am thankful that there is a keen interest in preserving the older varieties and discovering new ones. Now there are tomato tastings at farmers' markets, and people lined up with toothpicks stabbing chunks of ripe tomatoes— red currant tomatoes smaller than marbles, tomatoes that are green when ripe, pale yellow tomatoes, orange tomatoes, and a big red tomato called Radiator Charlie's Mortgage Lifter.

Paul Bertolli, the chef and co-owner of Oliveto restaurant in Oakland, thinks so highly of tomatoes that he offers tomato-based dinners at the height of the harvest. Someone attending one of these dinners could start with a tomato cocktail, such as a Bloody Mary; move on to cherry tomato parfait; sample semolina gnocchi with two tomato sauces; and then try a mixed roast of lamb with tomatoes cooked "around the clock" as a main course. The dinner need not end there, however. There's a choice of five tomato desserts (proving that tomatoes are really fruit, not vegetables), including frozen tomato soufflé and tomato ice cream.

Some catalogs sell seeds of heirloom tomatoes, and plants can be found at farmers' markets. Last year I bought two Brandywine plants and a Purple Calabash at the Boonville Farmers' Market. The leaves on the Brandywines, an Amish tomato from the nineteenth century, looked more like potato leaves than tomato, probably because they both belong to the same family, Solanaceae. The Brandywines were large fruits, pink at the stem end and darker underneath, with good texture and a taste balanced with just the right amount of acidity. The Purple Calabash plants produced the ugliest tomatoes I've ever seen: squat, knobby fruit with burnt-red tops and brownish bottoms. But once the thick skin was removed and they were sliced, their complex flavor redeemed them.

Following in my father's footsteps, I plant tomatoes, both heirlooms and hybrids, every year. I used to limit myself to three plants. Then one year I decided to start tomatoes from seed. Since only half of those seeds became viable plants, I more than doubled the seeds started the next year. All survived. I had seventeen plants in our country garden. In San Francisco, there were four in my vegetable plot, several more crowding out the roses, and others in pots growing tall and gangly while I searched for space to plant them. I gave plants away; my husband took them to the office.

The San Francisco weather isn't like Pittsburgh summers, so I haven't been able to replicate my father's tomatoes. Beefsteaks will never grow here. I keep trying new varieties, always hoping to capture that elusive taste.

Even the summer I grew that surplus crop, I didn't have enough tomatoes to "put up" for the winter. So, as in years past, I bought a box of canning tomatoes at a favorite farm stand. After a blanching and a brief cooking, I bottled them in a dozen pint jars, a mere gesture compared to my mother's multitudinous quarts. They're always gone by Christmas. Then, when I'm stuck for some tomato flavor to round out a stew or make a sauce for baked fish, I have to turn to the commercial canned variety. These are usually plum tomatoes, which are fleshier and withstand the rigors of commercial handling better than others. A new California company is packing organically grown tomatoes in white-enamel-lined cans, which eliminate that tinny taste. They seem to have more flavor, perhaps because they ripen on the vine. Although they suffice for cooked preparations, I still long for the juicy texture of fresh summer fruit.

I still eat fresh tomatoes only at the height of their season, be it my home-grown ones or fruit I buy at farmers' markets or at stores I trust to have only the best. In the middle of January, I walk past the pale pink imitations in grocery stores. I also pass up the frozen fish sticks.

Tomatoes Garnished with Tomatoes

At the height of the season, after you've eaten your fill of fresh tomatoes for the moment, make this fanciful dish and serve it as a first course for company. This was inspired by a recipe created by the Troisgros family, who operate a three-star restaurant in Roanne, France.

A minuscule amount of saffron adds taste, aroma, and color to whatever it touches. Two tips are important to bring out saffron's full flavor. First, carefully dry the strands in a skillet on top of the stove over medium heat, turning them with your fingers. When the skillet is too hot for your fingers, the saffron should be dry and brittle. Second, saffron needs to steep in hot and/or acidic liquid to fully bring out its flavor.

4 SERVINGS

> 8 meaty medium tomatoes, about 2¼ pounds
> ⅛ teaspoon saffron threads, dried as described above
> 2 tablespoons hot water
> 3 tablespoons olive oil, plus more for the baked tomatoes
> 2 cloves garlic, finely chopped
> 1 medium onion, finely chopped
> ½ teaspoon fennel seeds
> Salt and pepper

Peel and seed 4 of the tomatoes as follows: Bring a large pot of water to a boil. Cut out the stem end of the 4 tomatoes and drop them in the water. When the skin splits, immediately put them in a large bowl of cold water. The skin should then slip off easily. Cut the peeled tomatoes into halves through their equators. Grasp one half in the palm of your hand, squeeze slightly, and with a flick of the wrist remove the seeds. Repeat with the rest of the tomato halves. Coarsely chop them and set aside.

Preheat the oven to 400°F and warm 4 plates.

Steep the saffron in the hot water.

Heat the olive oil in a medium saucepan. Add the garlic and onions and cook until translucent but not browned. Add the saffron and water, the chopped tomatoes, the fennel seeds, and salt and pepper. Cover and cook over low heat until soft, 20 to 25 minutes, adding a little more water if necessary.

Cut the remaining 4 tomatoes into halves through their equators. Put them on a baking sheet, cut side up, season with salt and pepper, drizzle with olive oil, and bake until they are bubbling and soft but still maintain their shape, about 25 minutes. Remove the tomatoes from the oven. Spread a layer of the cooked tomato mixture on each of the serving plates. Place a baked tomato in the middle of each plate. Serve immediately with crusty bread.

Tomato and Sorrel Pizza

The citrus tang of sorrel goes well with the sweetness of garden-fresh tomatoes. Sorrel can sometimes be found in the herb section of grocery stores, and it's also easy to grow yourself. To make good pizza at home, be sure to have a thin crust, a hot oven, and a hot baking stone.

4 INDIVIDUAL PIZZAS

The pizza dough

1¾ cups (14 ounces) cold tap water
2½ teaspoons active dry yeast
4¼ cups (21 ounces) unbleached all-purpose flour
2½ teaspoons salt

The topping

4 handfuls fresh sorrel leaves, julienned
8 medium tomatoes (about 1½ pounds), thinly sliced
Salt and pepper
Good olive oil

Make the pizza dough

Pour the water into the bowl of a heavy-duty mixer. Sprinkle the yeast on the water and let it dissolve and become creamy, about 5 minutes. Add the flour and salt. Using a dough hook, knead on medium speed for 10 minutes, adding more water or flour as necessary so that the dough forms a ball. Cover the bowl with plastic wrap and let the dough rise at room temperature (75°F) until it doubles, about 2½ hours.

Shape and bake the pizza

Place a baking stone on the middle shelf of the oven and preheat it at 500°F for 45 minutes.

Turn the dough out onto a floured work surface. Divide it into 4 pieces. Shape each piece into a ball. Cover the balls with a kitchen towel and let rest for 5 minutes. Flatten one of the balls and gently stretch it into a 9-inch disk. You can do this by resting the dough on your fists and gently stretching it or by rotating the edge of the disk of dough in your hands. If the dough resists stretching, let it rest a few minutes, then try again.

Put the disk of dough on a well-floured baking peel or flat cookie sheet.

Sprinkle the sorrel on the dough, leaving a 1-inch margin around the edge. Cover the sorrel with a single layer of tomato slices. Season the tomatoes with salt and pepper. Drizzle olive oil over the top, making sure to put some on the exposed margin of dough. As you add the topping, shake the peel occasionally to make sure that the dough isn't sticking.

Slide the pizza onto the baking stone. Bake until the top is bubbling and the dough is browned, 10 to 15 minutes.

Repeat with the other dough rounds. If your oven is big enough, bake 2 or 3 pizzas at a time.

Remove the pizzas from the oven and serve immediately.

Pasta with
Fresh Tomatoes and Basil

The goodness of the tomatoes shines through in this dish because they're not cooked at all, proof that wonderfully fresh food doesn't need elaborate intervention. A simple technique of grating removes the skin from the tomato flesh. I first had a dish similar to this at a small restaurant in Florence several years ago.

4 SERVINGS

> *4 medium tomatoes (about 1 pound), the tastiest you can find*
> *2 tablespoons slivered basil, about 12 leaves*
> *12 ounces dried penne*
> *¼ cup (2 ounces) extra-virgin olive oil*
> *Salt and pepper*

Prepare the tomatoes

Cut each tomato into halves through its equator. Grasp one half in the palm of your hand, squeeze slightly, and press out the seeds with a flick of the wrist. Put the open bottom of a 4-sided grater in a bowl and rub the cut side of each tomato half up and down on the side with the largest holes. Keep your outstretched fingers flat on the tomato. Discard the tomato skin when it has surrendered its pulp. Add the slivered basil to the tomatoes.

Heat 4 individual serving bowls.

Cook and sauce the pasta

Bring 4 quarts of generously salted water to a boil. Add the pasta and give it a stir. Bring back to a rolling boil and cook until the pasta is al dente. Start tasting it after 5 minutes to be certain that it's not overcooked.

Drain the pasta and put it in the bowl with the tomatoes and basil. Add the olive oil, salt, and a few turns of black pepper, then toss everything together. The pasta should be lightly sauced in the Italian style, not swimming in tomato purée.

Divide the pasta among the warm bowls and serve immediately. If you have fresh garden greens, lightly dress them and serve them on the side.

Visions of Bakeries

I HAD A LONG LOVE AFFAIR WITH A MACHINE. Not the red 1967 Alfa Romeo that my husband gave me for our twentieth anniversary, not my green Lawn Boy rototiller that has churned up expanses of clay-packed soil, not even my trusty Flexible Flyer that carried me down snow-packed hills when I was a kid. The object of my affection was an electric dough sheeter. It was an apparatus with heavy steel rollers like the wringers on an old-fashioned washing machine, operated by a rocker switch attached to arms on either side. The rollers could be moved closer and closer together, so that they would flatten a block of dough to a thickness of ⅛ inch.

Shortly after opening the bakery, we were making too many tarts to roll the dough by hand, so I ordered the sheeter from France. It made a six-week journey from the outskirts of Paris to the San Francisco Airport. I couldn't just go and collect it; such an important item needed the escort of a customs broker to clear its passage into the country. A delivery service brought it to the bakery late one afternoon. We used a crowbar to dismantle the wooden crate and free it of its packing. Then we picked the sheeter up (it took three of us), put it on a work table, and stood back to admire our newcomer.

It was so much more chic, with its sleek Yves St. Laurent lines, than its American counterparts. Its finishing touches were regal—a gold-painted base set off with stainless steel arms, and a metal box on top, like a hat, to hold flour. Its beguiling litheness hid a workhorse soul, centered in those heavy rollers. Despite its might, it fit on a tabletop, unlike its domestic cousins, with their long, clumsy belts and everyday white finish, whose footprints demanded eight feet of precious floor space.

The sheeter freed us from the drudgery of rolling tart dough with rolling pins. It also led us to new horizons, helping me expand my vision of the bakery. Now we could make *croissants,* a task I couldn't face without it. A yeasted dough is flattened, slathered with butter, turned onto itself like a letter, and flattened again. This process is repeated three more times. The dough must cool and relax between these motions. It is a herculean effort without a machine. The sheeter made it simple. We put the steel plates in place at the bottom of the rollers to catch the dough as it went back and forth. Then we opened the rollers as wide as they would go and pushed the dough between them. A handle with a squeeze release moved the rollers closer; the dough went through again, left to right and back, getting thinner and longer. After all the turns were made, we brushed the flour from the sheeter. It rested overnight on the table while the dough cooled in the refrigerator. The next morning, the dough was flattened again, then cut with a *croissant* cutter I bought in Paris. The pieces were rolled onto themselves, allowed to rise, then baked to a dark brown in a hot oven. Others were cut into rectangles and baked with bars of French chocolate inside. They were wonderful—multiple layers of buttery goodness with a crisp outside, possible only because of the sheeter.

Making shortbread cookies was also a snap. We made two varieties: chocolate, almost black with cocoa powder; and vanilla, scented with Madagascar Bourbon vanilla. After the sheeter rolled the dough to a uniform ⅛ inch, we cut hearts or Easter bunnies or witches riding on broomsticks or Santas or, if it wasn't even close to a holiday, dinosaurs or rounds with scalloped edges. If some broke when we took them off the baking trays, we ate them, the bitterness of the cocoa tamed by sugar, both flavors buttery in our mouths.

What a performer! Year after year the sheeter was faithful. The oven switches broke regularly, the mixers stripped their gears, but the sheeter had only one episode of ill health—the switch that changed the rollers' direction quit. We could still use it, but we had to pick up the dough and feed it into the machine from the left side, the direction that was still intact. I called the company that serviced our equipment. They couldn't find a replacement part. "It's a French machine; no one carries the parts," they moaned. I found the manual that came with it and took the address of the French company to the service manager. He sent them a letter (I translated) requesting the broken piece. Someone from France called to verify the order, speaking perfect English. The part arrived and was installed. Once more the sheeter took on its dough-flattening tasks, humming as it worked. During the ten years I owned it, ten miles of dough must have passed through its gleaming rollers.

In the disorienting days after the fire at the bakery, the sheeter—which survived undamaged—pulled its weight once more and helped us over a difficult hurdle. A local catering company lent us their kitchen so we could bake for the Ferry Plaza Farmers' Market. But they didn't have a sheeter. We lugged ours to their kitchen, only to discover that its plug wouldn't fit into their sockets. I called our electrician, who arrived with the correct plug on Friday afternoon, just in time for us to make *croissant* dough. Appearing at the market on Saturday morning with our *croissants* and *pains au chocolat* let me believe that the bakery could still go on; it helped soothe the shock of what had happened. Then I found another temporary location, with a sheeter, where we baked for awhile, under trying conditions. I took my sheeter home and stored it in the basement.

Difficult months passed. The building that housed the bakery still wasn't ready. After many hours of soul-searching, I decided I didn't have the all-encompassing drive and commitment I knew would be necessary to start my bakery again. Something that special happens only once.

I sold all the other equipment, but I couldn't part with the sheeter. Its steadiness, continuity, and hard work embodied what the bakery had been. I loved it as much as I had loved the business. It sat in our basement on a table next to a toolbox, unused. I couldn't plug it in if I had wanted to; our house lacked an outlet with the requisite voltage. For two years, it gathered dust and was home to spiders.

Then one day at a meeting of the Bakers' Dozen, a group of baking enthusiasts, Elizabeth Falkner asked me if I had a sheeter for sale. She was opening a bakery soon and was scouting around for equipment. I hesitated.

"Ah, I do have a sheeter, but it's a small one, in my basement. I never use it. But I don't know if I want to sell it."

"Are you keeping it in case you open another bakery?" Elizabeth asked.

"No, I'm not planning to start another one."

"Well, think about it. I'd be interested, if you'll consider selling it," she said.

I went home and thought.

"Be rational," I told myself. "You're never going to use it again. Even if you wanted to, you'd have to run a separate electrical line. A rolling pin will be just fine for any dough work you want to do."

I asked Sidney for his opinion. Fully understanding my complex relationship with the machine, he wouldn't touch the subject. "It's up to you," was his only advice.

A few weeks went by. I realized that over the last year I hadn't thought of the sheeter very much, just as I hadn't thought much about the bakery. Maybe it was destined to be—the sheeter's special place in my heart was waning and Elizabeth really needed it. Letting her have it would let a shadow of my bakery live on. She was enthusiastic and determined, just as I had been when I started my business. She would give the sheeter a good home.

I took a deep breath and dialed her number. She came the next day and we struck a deal. But I got to keep the sheeter for a few more weeks while her space was under construction. She gave me a tour of the new bakery's space with its small espresso bar, a wood-burning oven erected by Alan Scott of Ovencrafters, and streamlined display cases for pastry. She and her business partner had renovated an old wooden building in an industrial part of the city, leaving arched skylights that let the sun shine through onto the minimalist decor. The tall facade of ground-to-ceiling windows in ironwork frames and huge wooden doors was set back from the street, leaving a concrete patio for outdoor tables and potted plants, which softened the look of the chain-link fence topped with barbed wire at the sidewalk that was secured when the bakery was closed.

Now, like visiting an old love from the past, I visit the sheeter at Citizen Cake. It's doing its job, judging from the *croissants* and the pistachio-studded crusts that support the rose-scented vanilla custard in the Rosebud Brûlée Tart. But when I'm there, the pastries with fanciful names make me forget the sheeter. Caramel Sutra, sponge cake soaked with coffee syrup, layered with caramel pastry cream, then covered with hazelnut buttercream, holds my attention. Orange-Creamsicle Cake tastes so much better than the frozen confection I ate as a child; just as S'more Brownies, with house-made marshmallows, elevate this campfire treat to another level. I bought an After Midnight Chocolate Cake for Sidney's birthday, a rich chocolate cake layered with milk chocolate mousse, then glazed with dark chocolate and decorated with thin chocolate shards.

But Citizen Cake isn't just for dashing in and picking up a dessert for dinner. It's a bakery in the middle of a vibrant city, an anchoring place for people to drop in and wash down a cinnamon roll with a cup of cappuccino while standing at the espresso bar or sitting on the patio. Or lunchgoers might arrive just in time for individual round pizzas coming out of the wood-fired oven, topped with sliced potatoes and an egg sunny-side up. There are many bakeries like this in European cities, places where everything is made and sold on the premises, hubs of activity that bring friends together. Every city needs them, both in Europe and here. In today's world of virtual realities, they help ground us. Warming cold hands with a cup of thick hot chocolate or eating a piece of perfect pastry are pleasures that make life more civilized, pleasures that will withstand the passage of time.

Elizabeth's ability to merge art with food was influenced by her parents. Her father is an abstract artist and her mother a good cook. "We often had soufflés for dinner. I thought that everybody had them," she said.

She attended Pepperdine University in Southern California, where her father teaches. After an exciting junior year in Europe, she knew she couldn't go back to conservative Pepperdine. Elizabeth moved north to

San Francisco to continue studying film at the San Francisco Art Institute. Her final film project, *Black Espresso, Black Sorbet,* foreshadowed what was to come. After graduation, she worked for a film production company. But it was while helping a friend in a restaurant kitchen that she stumbled into a pastry job. Masa's was looking for an assistant pastry chef; she walked up the street and applied. This is where she learned the basics of classical pastry and honed her skills, which eventually got her the position of pastry chef at Rubicon when Traci Des Jardins was the chef. The notion of opening her own place was kindled while she worked there. People often called the restaurant to order special cakes to take home. She realized there was a market for custom cakes. "Every day someone has a birthday in San Francisco," she told me.

The last time I was at Citizen Cake that someone was actress Sharon Stone, and Elizabeth was concocting a creation to help her celebrate. Elizabeth knit her eyebrows together under her spiked blonde hair as she contemplated recipes and ideas. The cake developed in stages, like a piece of sculpture: first she baked thin sheets of cake with hazelnuts, chocolate, and orange zest; then she decided on a hazelnut mousse to hold the layers together. She drew a picture of the finished pastry before she assembled it—a square enclosed in triangles of chocolate, with chocolate sticks and fancy sugar decorations jutting from the top.

Elizabeth sees pastry as art and wants to push it to another level, defying common notions of taste combinations and structure. She works with customers to conjure up unconventional cakes, drawing from classic French technique, American homey tastes, and a wide-open idea about how it's all assembled.

"Why do wedding cakes have to be so white and virginal?" she asks rhetorically. She does things I would never have dreamed of doing— peanut butter and grape jelly pastries, and chocolate truffles rolled in lavender sugar. When I let myself be open to the newness, these inventions taste good. She invites the challenge of creating edible architecture. And the taste must be as fantastic as the look.

I will head for Elizabeth's bakery when I need a cake for a special occasion or as a pause in the day for an afternoon sweet. And if I'm ever faced with a daunting baking project—lining lots of miniature tart pans with dough, or flattening pounds of puff pastry—I'll go to Citizen Cake and visit the sheeter. Elizabeth said I could use it anytime.

PEANUT BUTTER AND JELLY CAKE

from Citizen Cake

Thanks to Elizabeth Falkner for this playful recipe, letting us all be children again.

This is a simpler version of the cake constructed at the bakery, where it is often paired with chocolate or buttercream.

8 SERVINGS

The cake

> 1½ cups (7½ ounces) cake flour
> ¾ teaspoon baking powder
> ½ teaspoon baking soda
> ½ teaspoon salt
> 3 generous tablespoons (2½ ounces) creamy peanut butter
> 8 tablespoons (4 ounces) unsalted butter at room temperature
> ½ cup (3½ ounces) granulated sugar
> 1 cup (6 ounces) light brown sugar, packed
> 1 teaspoon vanilla extract
> 2 extra-large eggs at room temperature
> ⅔ cup (5 ounces) whole milk

The filling and topping

> ½ cup (8 ounces) good-quality jam (grape is traditional, but berry or another favorite may be used)
> 2 teaspoons creamy peanut butter
> 1 tablespoon powdered sugar
> 1 cup (8 ounces) heavy whipping cream

Bake the cake

Preheat the oven to 325°F.

Line a 17 x 11-inch baking pan with parchment paper.

Sift together flour, baking powder, baking soda, and salt and set aside.

Place the peanut butter, butter, and sugars in the bowl of a heavy-duty mixer. Beat with a paddle at medium speed until well combined. Add the vanilla and eggs all at once, and beat until the mixture thickens and is lighter in color. Add the dry ingredients and milk alternately, a third at a time.

Pour the batter into the baking pan and distribute it as evenly as possible with a spatula. (A metal offset spatula is the tool to use if you have one.) Bake it in the middle of the oven until a toothpick inserted into the center comes out clean, about 25 minutes. Cool the cake in its pan on a rack.

Assemble the "sandwiches"

Turn the cake out of the pan onto a work surface. Trim the edges and cut it into 16 pieces of equal size. Make "sandwiches" by spreading one piece with jam and topping it with another piece.

Whip the peanut butter, sugar, and heavy cream until soft peaks form. Spoon a dollop over each "sandwich" and serve.

STRAWBERRY ICE CREAM

from The Downtown Bakery and Creamery

The Downtown Bakery and Creamery, with its screen door that slaps closed, is located on the square in the rural town of Healdsburg, north of San Francisco. It is one of my favorite bakeries. The owners' original vision was to open an ice cream shop; then they decided to add baked goods as well. The ice cream is superb, egg-rich and silky smooth, fruit purées churned into some, caramel or nuts swirled into others. I am always tempted by the case holding buckets of ice cream at the bakery, and I have a hard time choosing between ice cream or a fruit *galette*.

Thanks to Kathleen Stewart for sharing this recipe. She often substitutes other fruits for the strawberries, such as peeled peaches, apricots, or other berries, using the same amount of purée and adjusting the sugar according to the sweetness of the fruit.

The custard needs to chill for several hours before freezing, so make it the day before or early in the morning of the day the ice cream is churned.

I QUART

The custard

⅔ cup (5 ounces) whole milk
⅓ cup (2½ ounces) granulated sugar
3 extra-large egg yolks
2 cups (16 ounces) heavy whipping cream

The fruit

1½ pint (about 3 cups) ripe strawberries
½ cup (3½ ounces) granulated sugar

Make the custard

Stir the milk and sugar in a medium nonreactive saucepan over medium heat until the sugar is dissolved, then bring to a boil. In a medium bowl, whisk the egg yolks. Gradually pour the hot milk into the yolks, continuing to whisk. Return this custard to the pan and cook over medium heat, whisking constantly, until the mixture is 160°F. The custard will thicken and coat the back of a spoon. Don't let it boil. Strain it into a large bowl or 1½-quart container. Stir in the cream, and refrigerate while preparing the fruit.

Prepare the fruit and make the ice cream

Wash and hull the berries, then purée them in a food processor. You should have 2 cups of purée. Put the purée in a nonreactive saucepan, add the sugar, and stir it over medium heat until the sugar is dissolved. Stir the fruit purée into the custard, and chill for at least 5 hours or overnight. Freeze the mixture in an ice cream maker according to the manufacturer's instructions.

Vanilla Bean Shortbread

from The Downtown Bakery and Creamery

Another thank-you to Kathleen Stewart, who knows that ice cream needs cookies.

These cookies can be enjoyed on their own, nibbled with a glass of lemonade or a cup of tea, or used to make decadent ice cream sandwiches. The dough can be refrigerated for 2 weeks or frozen for 1 month.

4 DOZEN COOKIES

4 cups (1¼ pounds) unbleached all-purpose flour
2 cups (14 ounces) granulated sugar
1½ teaspoons salt
1 vanilla bean
1 pound unsalted butter, refrigerator cold
2 extra-large egg yolks

Put the flour, sugar, and salt in the bowl of a heavy-duty mixer. Split the vanilla bean lengthwise with a paring knife. Using the dull side of the knife, scrape the seeds from the vanilla bean into the flour and sugar. Cut the butter into ½-inch cubes and add them to the bowl, mixing with the paddle at low speed until the flour and butter look like coarse cornmeal. Add the egg yolks and mix until the dough just comes together. Divide the dough into 3 portions on a lightly floured work surface. Shape each piece into a log, about 4½ inches long and 2½ inches in diameter. Wrap them in plastic and chill until firm.

Preheat the oven to 350°F.

Unwrap the logs and slice them into ¼-inch rounds. Place the rounds on parchment-lined baking sheets, 2 inches apart. Bake the cookies in the middle of the oven until the edges are golden, about 15 minutes. Cool them on a rack, then store them in an airtight container.

For ice cream sandwiches

    The sandwiches are easier to make if the ice cream isn't rock-hard, so let it sit at room temperature for a few minutes to soften it. Put a cookie, top side down, on a work surface. Put a scoop of ice cream on top, then cover with another cookie, top side up. Gently press down on the top cookie, being careful not to break it. Serve the sandwiches immediately or store them, wrapped in plastic, in the freezer.

Brioches with Goat Cheese Custard and Fruit

from Citizen Cake

This is one of the first things I tasted at Citizen Cake, Elizabeth Falkner's bakery. The fruit and honey add just the right touch of sweetness to the custard. I have made these with *fraises des bois* from my garden, and figs or apricots are equally wonderful.

The brioche dough needs to chill overnight, so make it the day before you plan to bake the pastries.

8 PASTRIES

The brioche dough

7 tablespoons (3½ ounces) unsalted butter at room temperature
¼ cup (2 ounces) whole milk, lukewarm
1¼ teaspoons active dry yeast
2 extra-large eggs at room temperature
1 teaspoon salt
2 tablespoons (1 ounce) granulated sugar
1½ cups (7½ ounces) unbleached all-purpose flour

The goat cheese custard

5 ounces fresh goat cheese (Cypress Grove Chevre is my favorite)
2 tablespoons (1 ounce) granulated sugar
2 teaspoons honey, plus more for drizzling over the finished pastries
1 tablespoon plus 2 teaspoons unbleached all-purpose flour
Pinch ground nutmeg
1 extra-large egg
½ teaspoon lemon juice
½ teaspoon Grand Marnier or cognac

The fruit

4 ripe figs or apricots, cut into halves, or a handful of fraises
des bois

Make the brioche dough

Beat the butter, either with a hand whisk or in a mixer, until creamy, and set aside.

Put the milk in the bowl of a heavy-duty mixer. Sprinkle the yeast over the milk and wait until the grains dissolve, about 5 minutes. Add the eggs, then the salt, sugar, and flour. Using a dough hook, mix the dough at low speed until all of the ingredients are combined, then knead it at medium speed for 8 minutes, adding more flour if the dough doesn't pull away from the sides of the bowl. This is a soft dough and won't completely clean the bottom of the bowl.

After 8 minutes, add the butter, a third at a time, waiting for the dough to incorporate each portion before continuing. Add very small quantities of flour if the dough sticks to the sides of the bowl. When the dough has absorbed all of the butter, remove the bowl from the mixer, cover it with plastic wrap, and let it rise at room temperature for 1 hour. Then punch it down, cover again, and refrigerate overnight.

Make the custard

Whisk the cheese, sugar, and honey together in a medium bowl. Whisk in the flour and nutmeg, then the egg, lemon juice, and Grand Marnier.

Assemble the pastries

Remove the brioche dough from the refrigerator and place it on a lightly floured surface. Divide it into 8 equal pieces, about 2 ounces each. Form each piece into a ball. Flatten each ball into a disk, and place the disks on a parchment-lined baking sheet. Make an indentation in each disk by pressing the back of a tablespoon into the center. Fill the indentations with the custard. Push a fig or apricot half into the custard, cut side up, or arrange a few *fraises des bois* on each one.

Place wine glasses upside down on the edges of the baking sheet to keep the rising dough from sticking to the plastic, and slip the sheet into a large plastic bag. Let rise in a warm (80°F) place until the pastries have risen by half, about 1 hour.

Bake the pastries

Preheat the oven to 375°F.

Slip the baking sheet out of the bag, remove the wine glasses, and place the sheet on the middle shelf of the oven. Bake until the brioche and custard are brown, about 20 minutes. Drizzle ½ teaspoon of honey over each pastry, and serve warm.

CHOCOLATE DREAMERS

ROBERT STEINBERG WAS LATE. The roasting cocoa beans were almost finished, but where was Robert? The roasting time is critical—not long enough and the resulting chocolate is too acidic, too long and the chocolate tastes burned. The worker roasting the beans that day had been tasting them at intervals, and although he thought they were finished, he wanted Robert's consensus. Just as he was about to decide on his own, Robert jumped from his car, dashed in, took a few beans out of a small scoop in the front of the roaster, removed the outside shell, and put the crumbled pieces in his mouth. He chewed them intently, then pronounced, "They're ready." Robert turned a few dials on the roaster, and within minutes cocoa beans tumbled into the round steel base of the machine. The noise was deafening; I was glad Robert had handed me ear protectors before the beans started to fall.

The cocoa beans had made a long journey to the roaster. Some were Trinitario beans from Papua, New Guinea, some Forastero beans from Ghana, others Criollo beans from other cocoa-bean-producing countries. All grew in pods hanging from trees grown close to the equator. Workers hand-picked them, then freed them from the pods using machetes. The beans, and the white pulp that surrounded them in the pods, sat in wooden boxes until they fermented, developing the precursors that are changed into chocolate flavor during roasting. Then they were spread on mats in the hot sun and dried before being shipped.

Four years ago, roasting cocoa beans was the last thing on Robert Steinberg's mind. He had sold his medical practice and become friends with Bob Voorhees, who owns three restaurants in San Francisco. The pair rekindled a dream Bob had fifteen years earlier—making chocolate. They visited Bernachon, a highly respected chocolate maker in France. The

Bernachons have been making chocolate since the 1940s, using small machines and carefully selecting cocoa beans from around the world. They turn the chocolate they make into deeply flavored confections and delicate pastries that they sell in their pastry shop in Lyon.

I can personally attest to the mastery of Bernachon chocolates. Once, on a brief stop during a family vacation, I experienced some of their creations: tiny towers of roasted hazelnuts covered with bittersweet chocolate that melted in my mouth before my teeth were through the nuts; *palets d'or*, coins of rich chocolate cream enclosed in a paper-thin covering of chocolate, then dusted with twenty-four-carat gold flecks that came off on my fingers before I could get the candy into my mouth; and balls with spiked exteriors, made to resemble chestnuts, with chocolate chestnut cream inside.

Their brief visit wasn't enough. Robert arranged for an apprenticeship at Bernachon. Once there, he helped roast beans, realizing that different beans require varying heat and times and that the only way to tell when they're ready is to taste, taste, taste. It was here that Robert decided that roasting is the most difficult and most important step in the process.

But it was the *mélangeur* that won his heart—a machine with two heavy granite rollers that crush the bits of shelled roasted beans, called nibs, into a coarse paste. The chocolate mass circulates in a rotating tub while the rollers mounted overhead slowly change its consistency. It is in this machine that the cocoa beans start to resemble chocolate. "When I saw the chocolate in the *mélangeur*, I knew this was something I had to do," he told me.

He returned home and realized that he had to find sources for beans. Just as the Bernachons gather beans from several countries, he knew he would have to do the same. Eventually he settled on eight sources.

Finding equipment was the next challenge. Chocolate manufacturers in this country have huge operations. The machinery available was far too large for what he had in mind. The search took him back to Europe, where he found a bright red roaster and *mélangeur* in Germany and, after considerable effort, a winnower in France.

Meanwhile, John Scharffenberger, who had founded a winery in the Anderson Valley that he had recently sold to a French company, joined the project. Bob Voorhees, realizing that the venture would require more attention than he could devote to it, withdrew to concentrate on his restaurants and an upcoming bakery.

The two entrepreneurs set up shop in an industrial district south of San Francisco. They named their company Scharffen Berger Chocolate Maker. Their vision is to produce hand-crafted chocolate as good as the best in Europe, using time-honored techniques. They are not interested in making confections, although their finished bars can be eaten out of hand. The transformation of cocoa beans into fine chocolate is their quest.

Next they turned their attention to the chocolate's production, a complicated process that fuses art and science. They worked on roasting technique, perfecting it by painstaking trial and error. The raw cocoa beans sit waiting in burlap sacks on pallets, just behind the roaster. Each variety requires a slightly different roasting, and each will impart its own flavor to the finished chocolate. The roaster heats and tumbles one variety at a time.

After roasting, the beans go to the winnower, where they are separated from their shells. Unlike the roaster, here the beans are treated equally. First they are poured into a hopper at one end of the machine. Little buckets attached to a chain transport them to the top and dump them onto a screen. Rollers attached to belts rub the beans against the screen, separating the beans from the shells. The chain rattles, the belts whir, the rollers crunch—it looks like something from the Middle Ages. The heavier nibs fall into tubs at the bottom, while the lighter shells are collected on the opposite side. The shells to go a local garden center. (The sharp shells make a good mulch that deters snails, the bane of every Bay Area gardener. Someone who mulched his garden with these spent shells told me that he thought Willy Wonka had moved his chocolate factory into his backyard.)

Bins of nibs are rolled to the next room, where the rest of the equipment waits. The air is heavy with a warm chocolate aroma. An international mix of nibs is poured into the *mélangeur* and dosed with sugar and vanilla to sweeten and flavor them. The heavy rollers slowly grind the pieces to a fine mush. The cocoa beans don't look like beans anymore. Now they look like grainy melted chocolate. But it takes two more steps to finish their transformation.

The dark paste is transferred to the *conche*, so called because the original machines were shaped like conch shells. (The one at Scharffen Berger resembles a cement mixer.) Cocoa butter is added to make the paste even more unctuous. Then the *conche* performs its mysterious role by heating, agitating, and aerating the mass. The specifics of how this changes the chocolate are not fully understood, but the process adds depth and finesse. Now the mix looks and tastes like melted chocolate. It needs to cool and return to a solid state for aging and shipping. Simply pouring it into molds won't work. Because the components of cocoa butter melt and solidify at different temperatures, chocolate must be heated and cooled in a precise fashion for the finished product to have the proper sheen and snap. The process is called tempering, and the machine that performs the task is a temperer. If the tempering is not done correctly, the finished bars streak and crack and have to be remelted.

There was trouble with the temperer the day of my visit. Robert looked frustrated. He conferred with two employees. They decided that the temperature of the machine wasn't right and made an adjustment. I appreciated their frustration. For a time at the bakery, we made large quantities of molded chocolates. At the beginning, we had trouble tempering the chocolate that lined the molds and had to remelt the finished candies and use them in a different way. Then, as now, the wrong temperature was the culprit.

The unmolded bars go to a small packing room, where they are painstakingly wrapped in heavy, foil-lined paper by workers wearing rubber gloves so that the chocolate isn't marred by fingerprints. They are then aged for sixty days before being shipped. The aging subdues the tannin and heightens the fruity taste of the chocolate.

The cocoa beans have now traveled thousands of miles. They have endured fermentation and drying in their native land and roasting, shelling, crushing, mixing, aerating, heating, and cooling in their new home. But they still wait in a state of suspended animation. Will a small bar be unwrapped by a chocolate lover in San Francisco and savored in small bites, or will that same bar be bought in a grocery store by a home baker, taken home, and melted and baked in a pound cake? Or maybe a three-kilo block will be delivered to a restaurant kitchen to become a batch of chocolate cakes. Or a chocolatier will buy the large blocks, melt them and temper them again, line jewel-like molds with a wafer-thin layer of chocolate, let it harden, fill the molds with a ganache made of the melted chocolate mixed with cream and Cognac, and then seal them with another thin layer of tempered chocolate. Then the chocolatier will pop the confections out of their molds, arrange them in fancy boxes and display them in a glass case to entice chocolate lovers. Regardless of how the exquisite chocolate is consumed, its flavor and intensity will set it apart from other chocolates. Then Robert Steinberg and John Scharffenberger will have realized their dream.

CHOCOLATE POUND CAKE

This is an old-fashioned pound cake, with the principal ingredients—butter, eggs, sugar, and flour—in almost equal proportion by weight. A bittersweet chocolate such as Scharffen Berger 70% is substituted for some of the butter, and chocolate chunks are added for more chocolate flavor. The result is a dense chocolate loaf.

For pound cake with a sauce, warm a slice of the cake just enough to slightly melt the chocolate bits, place it on a plate, and top it with ice cream, which will melt and soak into the cake.

1 CAKE

>7 ounces 70% bittersweet chocolate, chopped into ¼-inch chunks and divided into 2 portions—4 ounces and 3 ounces
>1 orange (only the zest will be used)
>1½ cups (7½ ounces) unbleached all-purpose flour
>¼ teaspoon salt
>1 teaspoon baking powder
>8 tablespoons (4 ounces) unsalted butter at room temperature
>1 cup (7 ounces) granulated sugar
>5 extra-large eggs at room temperature

Generously butter a loaf pan that measures 8½ x 4½ x 2½ inches.

Put 4 ounces of the chocolate in a bowl over a pan of simmering water and stir occasionally until it is melted. Remove the bowl from the pan of water and let the chocolate cool to room temperature. Zest the peel of the orange directly onto the remaining 3 ounces of chocolate chunks.

Preheat the oven to 350°F.

Sift together the flour, salt, and baking powder, and set aside.

Place the melted chocolate and butter in the bowl of a heavy-duty mixer. Beat with the paddle at medium speed until they are smooth. Gradually add the sugar and beat until everything is well combined.

In a separate bowl, beat the eggs with a fork to combine them. With the mixer on medium speed, dribble the eggs into the bowl, a little at a time, waiting after each addition until they are incorporated before adding more. Beat in the dry ingredients, a half at a time, then beat in the chocolate chunks and orange zest.

Pour the batter into the loaf pan and bake on the middle shelf of the oven until a skewer inserted into the middle comes out clean, about 1¼ hours. Watch closely after 1 hour to make sure the edges don't burn. Cool the cake, then remove it from the pan.

CHOCOLATE CHERRY TART

Scharffen Berger 70% bittersweet chocolate is the perfect foil for sweet Bing cherries. The cherry season is short, but don't be tempted by the first ones on the market. Wait until they are dark and sweet.

The dough needs to rest in the refrigerator for at least an hour before rolling, so make it ahead.

ONE 9-INCH TART, 8 SERVINGS

The tart dough

12 tablespoons (6 ounces) unsalted butter at room temperature
½ cup (3½ ounces) granulated sugar
1 extra-large egg
½ teaspoon vanilla extract
1¾ cups (8½ ounces) unbleached all-purpose flour

The filling

1 cup (8 ounces) heavy whipping cream
⅓ cup (2½ ounces) granulated sugar
5 ounces 70% bittersweet chocolate, finely chopped
1¼ pounds ripe Bing cherries
1 tablespoon kirsch
2 extra-large eggs

Make the tart dough

Place the butter in the bowl of a heavy-duty mixer. Beat at medium speed with the paddle until creamy. Add the sugar and beat until it is light and fluffy. In a separate bowl, beat the egg and vanilla together with a fork. With the mixer running, add the egg mixture to the butter mixture. Scrape the bowl and mix well. Add the flour all at once and mix just until it is incorporated. Remove the dough from the bowl, flatten it to a thickness of ½ inch on a piece of plastic wrap, cover with more plastic wrap, and refrigerate for 1 hour, or up to 3 days. The dough can also be frozen, tightly wrapped, for 1 month.

Assemble and bake the tart

Preheat the oven to 375°F.

Remove the dough from the refrigerator and roll it into a disk ⅛ inch thick on a lightly floured work surface. It should be larger than the tart pan. If the dough cracks and resists rolling, it is too cold. Let it warm a little, or pound it with a rolling pin to soften it. Transfer the dough to a fluted 9-inch tart pan that has a removable bottom and is 1 inch deep. Gently ease the dough into the bottom and up the sides of the pan. Run the rolling pin over the top edges of the pan to cut the dough. Chill it in the freezer for 10 minutes. Cover the dough with parchment paper, pressing it into the bottom edges. Fill the pan with rice or dried beans and bake on the middle shelf of the oven until the sides are lightly browned, about 10 minutes. Remove the beans and parchment paper, and return the pan to the oven until the bottom is set, another 5 minutes.

Put the cream and sugar in a medium saucepan. Whisk a few times to distribute the sugar, then bring the cream to a boil. Remove the pan from the heat. Add the chocolate and let it melt, whisking a few times. Cool the chocolate cream to room temperature.

Pit the cherries and toss them with the kirsch. Place them in the tart shell in one layer.

Beat the eggs into the cooled chocolate mixture and pour this over the cherries, making sure that all are covered.

Bake the tart on the middle shelf of the oven until the cherries are bubbling and the pastry is browned, 45 to 50 minutes. Cool to room temperature, remove from the tart pan, and slide onto a serving plate.

Chocolate Brioches with Chocolate Bits

A 70% bittersweet chocolate, such as Scharffen Berger, infuses this bread with chocolate flavor without sweetness. The chopped chocolate folded into the dough makes it even more chocolaty and adds a little crunch. Serve this sliced for breakfast.

Traditionally, brioche is made by beating butter into an egg-enriched dough. I have substituted chocolate for some of the butter in this recipe.

The dough chills overnight in the refrigerator, so make it a day before you plan to bake.

2 LOAVES

> 8 ounces bittersweet chocolate, finely chopped, divided into
>   2 equal portions
> 6 tablespoons (3 ounces) butter at room temperature
> ½ cup whole milk (4 ounces) warmed to room temperature
> 1 tablespoon active dry yeast
> 3 extra-large eggs at room temperature
> 2 teaspoons salt
> ¼ cup (2 ounces) granulated sugar
> 3 cups (15 ounces) unbleached all-purpose flour
> Egg wash: 1 egg mixed with 2 tablespoons water

Prepare the chocolate and butter

Put half of the chocolate in a metal bowl, then place the bowl over simmering water. (The remaining chocolate will be folded into the dough before baking.) When it has melted, remove the bowl from the heat and whisk in the butter. It should be the consistency of creamed butter. Set it aside while you make the dough.

Make the dough

Put the milk in the bowl of a heavy-duty mixer. Sprinkle the yeast over it and wait until the grains dissolve, about 5 minutes. Add the eggs, then the salt, sugar, and flour. Using a dough hook, mix the dough at medium speed until all the ingredients are combined, then knead it for 8 minutes, adding more flour if the dough doesn't pull away from the sides of the bowl. This is a soft dough and won't completely clean the bottom of the bowl.

After 8 minutes, add the chocolate/butter mixture, a third at a time. It should feel just warm to the touch, not hot. Wait for the dough to incorporate each portion before adding more. Resist the temptation to add more flour—it will make the final dough too stiff. When the dough has absorbed all of the chocolate/butter mixture and is an even chocolate color, remove the bowl from the mixer, cover it with plastic wrap, and let the dough rise at room temperature for 1 hour. Then punch it down, cover again, and refrigerate overnight.

Shape and bake the brioches

The next day, remove the dough from the refrigerator and let it warm up at room temperature for 3 hours.

Preheat the oven to 375°F.

Turn the dough onto a lightly floured work surface and divide it into 2 pieces. Divide the remaining 4 ounces of chocolate into 4 portions. Flatten one piece of dough into a rectangle about 10 x 6 inches. Sprinkle 1 portion of the chopped chocolate over the dough and roll it up. Flatten again, sprinkle with another portion of the chocolate, and roll up again. Let this dough rest while you roll the remaining chocolate into the other piece in the same fashion. Flatten each piece again, and roll each into a loaf. Place the loaves on a parchment-lined baking sheet, seam side down, and put the sheet inside a large plastic bag. Set tall glasses at the corners of the baking sheet so that the plastic won't stick to the rising loaves. Leave the loaves at room temperature until the dough has almost doubled, about 2 hours.

Remove the plastic bag and the glasses, and brush each loaf with the egg wash. Place the loaves on the middle shelf of the oven and bake until they are browned and hollow-sounding when tapped on the bottom, about 35 minutes. Cool the brioches on a rack.

Chocolate Pots de Creme

Use an intensely flavored chocolate to make this dessert. The result is a thick, creamy custard that is very smooth. A dollop of whipped cream would make it even more decadent.

Eight 6-ounce ramekins

2 cups (16 ounces) whole milk
2 cups (16 ounces) heavy whipping cream
½ cup (3½ ounces) granulated sugar
10 ounces bittersweet chocolate, such as Scharffen Berger or
*   Valrhona, finely chopped*
8 extra-large egg yolks
2 extra-large eggs

Preheat the oven to 325°F.

Bring the milk, cream, and sugar to a boil. Turn off the heat, add the chocolate, and whisk until melted. Cool to lukewarm.

In a medium bowl, whisk the yolks and eggs together. Whisk in the cooled chocolate mixture. Pour it through a sieve into a pitcher and divide among eight 6-ounce ramekins.

Make a *bain-marie*: Bring a large pot of water to a boil. Place the filled ramekins in a large baking pan. Pour boiling water into the pan until it comes halfway up the sides of the ramekins. Cover the pan with foil. Bake until the custards are just set, 50 to 60 minutes. They will still jiggle in the center. Remove the ramekins from the *bain-marie*, let them cool, then refrigerate them until serving.

Serve the custards with a dusting of powdered sugar or with a dollop of whipped cream.

BURIED TREASURE

I SHOULD HAVE WORN SIDNEY'S AUSTRALIAN OIL-CLOTH RAINCOAT and hat, but I was in a hurry. Mindful of the gray clouds and imminent rain, I headed to the garden—fifty feet, but a longer walk—below our country house, clutching a bucket, shovel, and hand trowel. By the time I got there, a fine mist brushed my face. "Not too wet; this won't take long," I thought as I went straight to the potato patch. But the nearby red-wood trees had sent forth substantial roots that wrapped around the tubers. It was hard work getting the potatoes from the heavy earth. As the mist turned to steady rain, I thought, "Only a few more—but wait, I haven't dug any of the Garnet Chiles, the ones we liked so much." Back to the muck with my shovel. Rain was running down my glasses, and my sweatshirt was soaked through. The treads on my boots were clogged with mud, requiring more effort to push in the shovel. Finally, I had enough potatoes and enough rain. I climbed back to the house and washed the mud from my spuds under a hose.

It was the potatoes I bought at a farmers' market some years ago that made me look at this staple in new light. What I remember most was their earthiness. I wanted to plant some immediately, but the plants needed more room than my San Francisco garden had available. Then we built our country house with a more spacious garden. I ordered a catalog from Ronniger's Seed & Potato Company in Idaho, now renamed Irish Eyes with a Hint of Garlic. The small, homey pamphlet was packed with infor-mation. I didn't know that potatoes matured at different rates—they were listed as early, mid, late-season, and fingerlings. And I had no idea there were sixty varieties. (Ronniger's is conservative; the Seed Savers Exchange maintains eight hundred.) The descriptions read like a history book: Caribe, brought from South America to the Caribbean by the Spanish;

Kerr's Pink, an old Irish variety introduced in 1917; Augsburg Gold, an heirloom preserved in a customer's family for generations; Sierra, developed at the University of California; Ozette, carried from Peru to Washington in the 1700s by Spanish explorers. Some were for roasting, others for boiling and mashing. It was difficult to choose; I finally settled on four. Each year I try a new group. So far, our favorites are Garnet Chile and German Butterball.

Every dinner during my childhood featured potatoes, usually peeled and boiled, and they weren't any of the ones named above. On special occasions my mother baked or mashed them. I took them for granted; they were a staple that soaked up the gravy from the braised round steak or meat loaf that we often ate. Three of my grandparents immigrated from Ireland, bringing the potato tradition with them, and my parents did their part to uphold it. Maybe there's an Irish potato gene that's responsible for potatoes being one of my favorite vegetables.

It was in Brussels that I ate the most decadent potato preparation (although Gerald Hirigoyen's potato gratin at his restaurant Fringale, made with ample cream and butter, runs a close second). Vendors sold *pommes frites* at stands on street corners and at road intersections. Not content just to sprinkle salt on their fries, the Belgians spooned on flavored mayonnaise, as if the frying hadn't raised their fat content enough. We ate them at every opportunity.

There are three types of potato that have been available for as long as I remember—Russets for baking, and white and red for boiling. Sometime in the last fifteen years or so, new varieties started showing up in farmers' markets. Actually, they weren't all new. Many had ancestors harking back thousands of years to the Andes, where they thrived at elevations that wouldn't sustain corn. Plant breeders have developed new varieties during the last century. "There are potatoes that have numbers, like social security numbers, instead of names," a vendor at a farmers' market told me.

Luther Burbank hybridized the Russet Burbank, and it still accounts for a third of the potatoes grown in Idaho. The names Russet and baking potato have become synonymous. But the poor boiling potatoes have lost their identity; two produce vendors couldn't name their varieties when I asked recently. I called the distribution center of a prominent West Coast supermarket and was referred to its public relations arm. They didn't know either but promised to investigate. After some delay, they sent me a list of varieties—Red LaSoda, Chieftain, Cherry Red, A79548, Cal White, Tejon, Cascade, and White Rose. In the stores, however, they're simply labeled "red" or "white."

In the Bay Area, a confluence of divergent interests supported the potato revival. The biodynamic/French Intensive method of organic gardening gathered a following. Alan Chadwick, a colorful horticulturist, started a garden adhering to those principles at the new campus of the University of California at Santa Cruz in 1967. John Jeavons, one of his disciples, carried on his work at Ecology Action of the Mid-Peninsula, a nonprofit environmental research and education organization, and in 1974 published a book, *How to Grow More Vegetables*, now in its fifth edition. I have a copy of the 1979 version.

Small growers became interested in heirloom potato varieties, seeking a diversity of crops in their gardens. Others wanted to become self-sufficient and grow their own food, and some, like Ina Chun, with a background in art history, migrated to farming from more academic pursuits. Soon she was growing more than she could eat and started selling produce from her farm, Ocean Resources at Ohana Ranch, to restaurants. The chefs who bought her potatoes, at Chez Panisse, the Balboa Cafe, Oliveto, and L'Avenue, wanted fresh, new, exciting produce to fulfill their imaginative bents. Potatoes with blue flesh, or marble-size potatoes, or potatoes shaped like gnarled fingers were so much more interesting than the standard varieties. And the taste! Instead of tired, cold-storage potatoes, these special specimens traveled from the ground to the table in twenty-four hours, delivering that earthy flavor, with each variety possessing its own nuances. I was compelled to plant my own.

The Bernstein family was also compelled to plant a few acres of potatoes at their property, Joshua Farms, north of San Francisco. Although much of their time is devoted to raising and training competition cutting horses, they had two acres of potatoes in the ground in a recent year—Caribe, a potato with purple skin and white flesh, which Lynn Bernstein loves to mash; Yellow Finn, good cooked a variety of ways; and two fingerlings. When I visited that June, a few of the plants had just started to flower. It would be another forty days before they took some to farmers' markets in San Francisco and sold others to a wholesale produce company.

The Bernsteins have found equipment suited to small plantings, but not without difficulty. A potato cutter, which cuts the seed potatoes into plantable pieces, reminded me of the winnower at Scharffen Berger Chocolate Maker, with its rattling chains and chutes. They found this machine in Pennsylvania. The seed potatoes are cut, then transferred to a hopper hooked up to the tractor. Two seats are just below the hopper, with tilted disks that resemble roulette wheels mounted in front between the hopper and the seats. Blades and shovel-like pieces below cut the earth, then cover the seeds. As the tractor advances, the roulette wheels spin, dropping the potatoes to the ground. The riders in the seats pick up potato chunks from the hopper and put one in each section of the wheel. What could be a leisurely drive through the field becomes a steely test of hand-eye coordination—the wheels spin rapidly. "It's not as easy as it sounds," said Lynn. "I tried to pick up several seeds in each hand, then drop them into the wheel, but I got behind." The empty slots produce uneven rows; instead of twelve inches between plants, one missing seed extends that space to twenty-four inches. I was reminded of a summer job working in an ice cream packing plant during my college years, picking up frozen confections, four in each hand, from a conveyer belt, and stacking them into waiting boxes. One mistake and the chocolate-covered bars piled up or spilled on the floor. It wasn't a job I wanted the rest of my life.

Philippa Spickerman, who was the chef at the Balboa Cafe for twelve years, has helped the Bernsteins realize the full potential of their crop. "We didn't know anyone wanted marble-size potatoes. Philippa was appalled when she saw us throwing them away," said Lynn. Chefs also like the fingerlings, to sauté or to roast. They don't pare them; the thin skins add to the taste. At Zuni Cafe, I've had fingerlings roasted in the wood-burning oven along with tender pieces of local salmon. I'm starting to salivate thinking about it.

The potato revival is elevating an old staple to a new status. But the chefs aren't inventing new, wild ways to cook them. They stick to simple preparations, letting the potatoes' true virtues—their texture and taste—shine. Potatoes are simple food, simply served.

Carlos Corredor, the chef/owner of Timo's, a tapas restaurant in the Mission District of San Francisco, understands potatoes. They aren't used as an addition to the plate, they are the plate. One could make a meal of them here; I have. In the simplest of preparations, he roasts small, red-skinned new potatoes and serves them with a mayonnaise so infused with garlic that it oozes from the pores the next day. Maybe he has Belgian ancestors. He also makes a classic *tortilla a la Española*, proving that good potatoes need only onions, olive oil, and enough eggs to hold them together to make a dish that is more than the sum of its parts. Yukon Golds get a special treatment at his restaurant—cooked with earthy wild mushrooms that intensify the potatoes' taste; he fittingly calls the dish Potato Decadence. Only Yukon Golds will do for the decadence, and he won't make the dish if he can't get them.

The two yellow varieties, Yellow Finn and Yukon Gold, are usually identified by name, even in large supermarkets. Maybe these two are the spuds of the future. (Ronniger's catalog named Yellow Finn as its best-selling variety in 1998.) If they are, I hope they keep their identity and aren't degraded to being called merely "yellow" potatoes.

GRATIN DAUPHINOIS

I saw Jean Pierre Bruneau prepare his version of this classic dish many times when I watched him cook in his Brussels restaurant kitchen. Cooking the potatoes before baking is the secret. The potatoes give off their liquid during this first step so that the final gratin is creamy instead of watery. When I first made this dish many years ago, I used generic "white" potatoes. Now I prefer Yukon Golds.

Jane Grigson reminds us how these potatoes got their name. The dish is from the Dauphiné region of France, which borders Italy and runs down to the Rhône river. It was added to France in 1349 and became the property of the king's eldest son. From then on, the king's eldest son became known as the Dauphin.

This hearty dish calls for roasted meat, perhaps a leg of lamb with garlic slivers inserted into the meat before roasting.

I cut the potatoes on my mandoline, but a food processor with a fine cutting blade or a sharp knife will also do the job.

6 SERVINGS

> 2 pounds Yukon Gold or white potatoes, peeled and sliced
> ⅛ inch thick
> 1 shallot, minced
> About 2 cups (16 ounces) whole milk
> 1 teaspoon salt
> ⅛ teaspoon white pepper
> 1 clove garlic, cut in half
> About ½ cup (4 ounces) heavy whipping cream
> Imported Parmesan or dry Jack cheese

Place the potato slices and shallot in a 9-inch skillet or sauté pan and add enough milk to almost cover the potatoes. Add the salt and pepper.

Bring the milk to a simmer, cover the pot with the lid slightly ajar, and cook over low heat, stirring frequently to keep the potatoes from sticking. The liquid will bubble and thicken. Cook until the potatoes just yield to the tip of a knife, about 10 minutes. Don't cook them until they fall apart.

Preheat the oven to 425°F.

Rub a 10 x 8-inch gratin dish with the cut side of the garlic clove. Using a slotted spoon, transfer the potatoes to the gratin dish, leaving behind any liquid that doesn't adhere to the potatoes. Pour cream over the potatoes so that they are about three-fourths covered. Grate a fine layer of cheese over the top.

Bake in the middle of the oven until the top is browned and bubbling, about 25 minutes.

POTATOES BAKED IN PARCHMENT

Annie Somerville of Greens restaurant in San Francisco gave me this idea. She often pairs the potatoes with other seasonal vegetables—she mentioned baby leeks and artichokes to me. This recipe is for the potatoes by themselves. Add other vegetables as you like, but choose those that will cook in the same amount of time as the potatoes.

It's fun to mix different colored potatoes. I used All Red, Bintje (white), and Purple (almost blue) for a Fourth of July party.

4 TO 6 SERVINGS

1 pound golf-ball-size potatoes
½ teaspoon fresh thyme leaves
Leaves from 4 sprigs flat-leaf parsley
3 cloves garlic, peeled
1 shallot, peeled and minced
¾ teaspoon salt
Several grinds black pepper
1 tablespoon olive oil

Preheat the oven to 425°F.

Mix the washed but unpeeled potatoes with the rest of the ingredients in a large bowl, then put them in the middle of a large piece of parchment paper. Fold the paper over the potatoes to make a compact package. Put the package on a baking sheet and bake in the middle of the oven until the potatoes can be pierced with a skewer, 30 to 35 minutes. Open the parchment and serve.

POTATO SALAD
WITH SAKE AND OLIVE OIL

A trick I learned from *Simca's Cuisine* by Simone Beck is to toss cooked potatoes that are still warm with white wine before using them in a salad. In the past, I've used vermouth, but I recently discovered that sake imparts a faint woodsy taste to the salad. After experimenting with a few sakes, I have settled on Sho Chiku Bai made by Takara in Berkeley. Leave the potato skins on; depending on the variety, they will either adhere or slip off easily after boiling.

I have used All Red and Red Norland potatoes for this salad with equal success.

6 SERVINGS

    2 pounds waxy potatoes
    ¼ cup (2 ounces) sake
    1 teaspoon salt
    Several grinds black pepper
    2 tablespoons snipped chives
    ¼ cup (2 ounces) extra-virgin olive oil

Put the potatoes in a large pot and cover them with salted water. Bring the water to a boil and cook until the potatoes can be pierced with a skewer. Drain. As soon as they are cool enough to handle, slice them. If the skins slip off, remove them; otherwise leave them intact.

Place the sliced potatoes in a bowl and pour the sake over them, tossing them gently. The potatoes will absorb the sake. Some may break into smaller pieces. Add the salt, pepper, chives, and olive oil and toss again. This salad is equally tasty served warm or at room temperature.

POTATO TOURTE

Potatoes baked in a savory crust, studded with flecks of black olives and flavored with garlic and scallions make this tourte an excellent choice for lunch or a dinner first course. It is sturdy enough to take on a picnic. If budget isn't a constraint, use pieces of black truffles instead of the olives. Choose waxy potatoes that will hold their shape during the baking.

A mandoline or food processor makes slicing the potatoes easy, or you can use a knife.

The dough for this tourte needs to be chilled before rolling, so make it at least an hour ahead.

ONE 9-INCH TOURTE, 6 TO 8 SERVINGS

The tourte dough
> 1¾ cups (8¾ ounces) all-purpose flour
> ½ teaspoon salt
> 10 tablespoons (5 ounces) unsalted butter, chilled
> 6 tablespoons (3 ounces) cold water

The filling
> 2 pounds waxy potatoes
> 1 teaspoon salt
> 1 ounce (about 8) black salt-cured olives, pitted and chopped
> 2 cloves garlic, minced
> 2 scallions, finely chopped
> Several grinds black pepper
> ⅓ cup (4 ounces) sour cream
> Egg wash: 1 egg mixed with 1 tablespoon of water

Make the tourte dough

Toss the flour and salt together in a medium bowl.

Cut the butter into ½-inch cubes. Add to the bowl with the flour.

Using your fingertips, rub the butter and flour together, scooping flour from the bottom of the bowl. The butter pieces will break into smaller, irregular pieces. Continue until the mixture looks like a coarse meal. The butter and flour will be mixed together, but each will stay a separate entity. The butter should not melt.

Add the water, a tablespoon at a time, while mixing with the other hand. Depending on the flour absorption, you may not need all of the water. It's better to have the dough on the dry side than too wet.

Turn the shaggy mass out onto a work surface and knead it a few turns until it comes together. It may still look a little rough. Shape it into a ball, flatten it to a ½-inch-thick disk with your hand, wrap it in plastic, and refrigerate for at least 1 hour, or up to 3 or 4 days. It can also be frozen.

Assemble and bake the tourte

Preheat the oven to 400°F.

Remove the dough from the refrigerator and put it on a lightly floured work surface. Roll it into a disk ⅛ inch thick. It should be larger than the tart pan. Roll the scraps into a flat disk; this will be the top. Transfer the dough to a fluted 9-inch tart pan that has a removable bottom and is 1 inch deep. Gently ease the dough into the bottom and up the sides of the pan. Run the rolling pin over the top edges of the pan to cut the dough. Refrigerate the tourte shell while you prepare the filling.

Peel and slice the potatoes ⅛ inch thick. Place them in a large bowl. Add the salt, olives, garlic, scallions, pepper, and sour cream, and mix everything together.

Pile the filling into the tourte shell. It will dome above the top. Roll the reserved dough into a circle ⅛ inch thick and about 2 inches larger than the tart pan. Fold it in half and make 4 diagonal cuts, about 1 inch long, through the center of the crease. Unfold over the potatoes. Use scissors to trim it so that it extends about ½ inch beyond the edge of the tart pan. Fold the edges to the inside of the pan, sealing the top and bottom together. Brush the top with egg wash.

Bake the tourte in the middle of the oven until the pastry is browned and the potatoes yield to the point of a knife, about 1 hour. When cool enough to handle, remove it from the tart pan. Serve the tourte warm or at room temperature.

Lobsters in the Lake

CRAYFISH, CRAWDADS, ÉCREVISSES, MUDBUGS—by any name, these small lobster look-alikes that live in fresh water instead of the salty seas make good eating. In this country, the crayfish capital is Louisiana, where they are the star of Cajun cooking, combined with okra in gumbo or with rice in jambalaya or made into Cajun popcorn, deep-fried morsels of tail meat, sprinkled with salt and popped into the mouth. But I wasn't in New Orleans the day I saw a large container of lively crayfish being protected from the sun by a wet burlap bag. I was in San Francisco at the Ferry Plaza Farmers' Market, where Jackie and Curtis Hagen were selling crayfish that had crawled into their traps twenty feet underwater in the Sacramento River.

Seeing the crustaceans brought back a flood of memories. When Sidney and I lived in Brussels, crayfish were the darlings of chefs cooking both haute and nouvelle cuisine. The tails were tossed with baby lettuce in salads, the shells were cooked with aromatics and strained to make bisque, the sweetness of their meat was spiced with curry. The French called them *pattes rouges*, a distinction I didn't understand—something to do with a particular species, I guessed. I never cooked crayfish in Brussels, and I can't remember even seeing any for sale, but we ate our share in restaurants.

Bay Area restaurants serve crayfish too, but they often buy only the tails from their fish suppliers. Carta, a restaurant in San Francisco with a menu that changes monthly, featured pickled crayfish the month they were cooking Southern fare. After a brief cooking, crayfish tails were marinated in a brine with vinegar and fistfuls of herbs—parsley, coriander seeds, dill, tarragon, and chiles. Just before serving, the fish were removed from the marinade and mixed with cubes of cucumber and avocado, then served in a goblet with Louis dressing. Lalime in Berkeley does serve whole crayfish, either boiled and paired with aioli or deep-fried, and they let the customers do the peeling. They also make a bisque, deep in flavor from the cooked shells. There's another restaurant in San Francisco called Yabbies, the Aboriginal name for crayfish, and yes, they serve them.

When we moved home to San Francisco from Brussels, crayfish weren't on my mind the day I took my two preschoolers to the de Young Museum for a special children's art show. They were fidgeting in line, impatient to get in, waiting beside a large round pool near the front door. A few feet away, a boy dangled a string into the water, pulling it out with flourishes as if he were fishing. After an especially big yank, the end of the string cleared the water to reveal a tiny crayfish clinging to the end. Casey was mesmerized. He ran to the boy and watched awestruck as he cast his string again and again into the water. Any interest Casey had in the art show paled in comparison to the miracle happening before him. When we finally entered the museum, his thoughts weren't on the art; all he could talk about was the crayfish.

Years later, we rented a house on Lake Almanor, near Lassen Park northeast of San Francisco. Although many people go there for the fishing, our purpose was to relax and play in the water—until we saw a crayfish trap for sale in the general store. Fishing license in hand, and tips from the locals duly noted, we headed back to the house to start our crayfish trapping career. At dusk, we rowed our small boat twenty-five feet offshore to a big underwater rock, tossed the trap in the water, and marked the line that led to it with an empty plastic bottle. Then we went to bed. The next morning, the kids leading the way, we climbed into the boat and rowed to the buoy. Casey, by this time ten years old, struggled to pull in the rope, hand over hand. Astonishment crossed his face when the trap came to the surface. It was full. We all cheered and rowed to shore. I found a large pot, brought water to a boil with a bay leaf and other spices unearthed in the cupboard, and cooked the crayfish. Then I reserved the tail meat, made a broth from the shells, and tossed all with pasta for dinner. Maybe the adventure of catching them contributed to their taste and acceptance—Casey and even Claire, who has since put all fish into the inedible category, cleaned their plates.

Back at the farmers' market, the pressing issue was how many pounds to buy. It was the Fourth of July, and we were grilling for a group of friends. A few boiled crayfish would stave off hunger as we cooked everything else, so I bought two pounds. I also arranged to visit Jackie's boat the next week.

When I asked her what time I should arrive, I was braced for the response—probably 5:00 A.M., I thought, necessitating a 3:00 A.M. departure from San Francisco. "What time do you want to come?" Jackie asked. "We can go out anytime. I'm my own boss." We decided on the leisurely hour of 10:00 A.M.

I drove against the commute traffic across the Bay Bridge and north on Interstate 80. At Fairfield, a two-lane road carried me east, through a plain. Just after a drawbridge that spans the Sacramento River at Rio Vista, I turned north onto a levee road that winds with the river, water on one side and cornfields and orchards on the other. In places the orchards were below the water level, with only the built-up road to keep them from flooding. It reminded me of a road that twisted along a canal near Bruges, Belgium, traveled by food lovers making the pilgrimage to Le Siphon, a restaurant noted for its eel in chervil sauce. This time my quest was for crayfish, not eels. Although the location is just a suburban distance from Sacramento, the setting is rural, anchored by the hamlet of Courtland and its picturesque town hall instead of a shopping mall.

Jackie's husband, Curtis, started crayfishing almost twenty-five years ago, and she joined him in 1980. During those early years, most of the fish were cooked and then sent to Scandinavia packed in a dill brine. Even today, Jackie has many Scandinavian customers who eat these dill-infused crayfish, washed down with aquavit. The overseas market collapsed in the early 1980s, the exchange rate driving the lucrative price too low to continue. The fishermen who remained formed a co-op, but solitary people looking out for their own interests aren't a good foundation for such an arrangement, so it only lasted about four years. Now there are only a handful of boats on the river, and many of their pilots are reclusive. Jackie Hagen is not. She greeted me enthusiastically, and we climbed into her big pickup, accompanied by her daughter, Penny, who was her fishing partner that summer. Both Jackie and Curtis still have "day jobs." She works for the U.S. Fish and Wildlife Service, tracking juvenile salmon, and Curtis works for the California Fish and Game Department. Jackie's job dovetails nicely with the fishing; during crayfish season, she works part-time. Although some people fish year-round, the Hagens stop in the fall, when the females carry fertilized eggs on their abdomens. "We call the eggs berries, and it's illegal to take females carrying eggs. We have to turn over every crayfish to look for eggs, and it slows down the process too much, so we stop for the winter," said Jackie. "It gives both the fish and us a rest."

We reached the dock and boarded their boat, the *Yabby*. Jackie explained that they would "pull a line," meaning empty and reset one of six strings of traps lying on the river floor. They had one hundred traps in the water; at the height of the season, that number would double. Jackie drove to the buoy, a plastic bottle reminiscent of the one at Lake Almanor. Penny caught the end of the line and attached it to a hydraulic hoist, which reeled in the traps as the boat slowly advanced. She unhooked the traps from the cable and handed them to Jackie, who opened them and dumped the crayfish onto a grate hanging from the side of the boat. Crayfish too small to harvest, less than 3⅝ inches, dropped through the grate to the river. Jackie tipped the grate upright and, with rubber-gloved hands, pushed the crayfish into a chute, which funneled them into a plastic container. A continual spray of river water from two nozzles bathed them. "You have to keep them cold and wet. They'll live happily on the bottom of the refrigerator, covered with wet towels, for two or three days," she said.

She picked another spot in the river, starting under a drawbridge, and reversed the process, hooking the traps to the cable and laying them on the bottom. She will pull them up in about forty-eight hours, and no longer than seventy-two, which is the legal limit.

This batch of crayfish was destined for the Marin County Farmers' Market the next morning, supplemented by others she would pluck from traps on another line later in the afternoon. They sell their entire catch at three farmers' markets, often 250 pounds at a time. We returned to the house and put the crayfish in a basement refrigerator, but not before we transferred eight pounds into my waiting cooler.

I retraced my drive along the winding levee, thinking of recipes. The simplest is the crayfish boil, cooking them in seasoned water until they just turn red, then letting the eaters shell them and crack the larger claws to extract the succulent meat. This is a messy endeavor, best accomplished outside at a picnic table, with plenty of napkins. I also planned to try the Scandinavian recipe Jackie recited to me on the return trip to her house.

GazPacho with Crayfish

The classic Spanish cold vegetable soup is dressed up with cooked crayfish meat, making it an elegant first course for a special summer dinner. A recipe in Georges Blanc's book, *Ma Cuisine des Saisons*, inspired this dish.

4 TO 6 SERVINGS

The crayfish

> 2 gallons water
> 5 sprigs fresh parsley
> 6 black peppercorns
> 2 bay leaves
> 2 teaspoons salt
> 2 small dried red chiles
> 2 pounds live crayfish

The gazpacho

> 1 large red bell pepper
> 2 tablespoons olive oil
> 1 shallot, minced
> 1 small onion, minced
> 2 garlic cloves, minced
> 2 pounds Roma or other paste tomatoes, peeled, seeded, and chopped
> 1 large cucumber, peeled, seeded, and sliced
> Dash cayenne pepper
> Leaves from three sprigs fresh thyme
> 1½ teaspoons salt
> Few grinds black pepper
> About ½ cup water
> 1 tablespoon extra-virgin olive oil
> 1 teaspoon red wine vinegar
> 2 slices good-quality bread, cubed and toasted

Cook the crayfish

Bring the water to a boil with the parsley, peppercorns, bay leaves, salt, and chiles. Add the crayfish all at once and cook until they turn red, about 3 minutes. Drain. When they are cool enough to handle, remove the tail meat from the shells, as well as the meat from any large claws. Refrigerate until serving time.

If you wish, make a stock for another use: Return the shells and bodies to the pot, cover with water, and simmer for 20 minutes. Strain and refrigerate when cool.

Make the gazpacho

Roast the pepper over a gas stove burner or under a broiler until the skin is charred. Put it in a paper bag until cool, then remove the skin under running water. Discard the stem, seeds, and ribs. Roughly chop the pepper and set aside.

Heat the olive oil in a small skillet. Cook the shallot, onion, and garlic until soft but not brown. Set aside.

Purée the tomatoes in a food processor fitted with a steel blade, and pour them into a large bowl.

Place the red pepper, cooked vegetables, cucumber, cayenne, thyme, salt, and black pepper in the food processor and, with the processor running, add enough of the water to make a purée. Stir this mixture into the tomatoes. Add the olive oil and vinegar, and taste for seasoning.

Refrigerate the gazpacho for at least 1 hour.

Serve the gazpacho

Ladle the gazpacho into individual serving bowls. Divide the crayfish meat among the bowls, and sprinkle the toasted bread cubes on top.

SCANDINAVIAN MARINATED CRAYFISH WITH DILL

Jackie Hagen recited this recipe as we drove back to her house after collecting crayfish from her traps. During the early years of her business, when the exchange rate favored exports, many crayfish were cooked, marinated in this brine, and then shipped to Scandinavia, where they were eaten in prodigious quantities, washed down with aquavit.

If you can't find crown dill, substitute four dill sprigs and a tablespoon of dried dill seeds. I used coarse sea salt imported from France to make the marinade.

4 APPETIZER SERVINGS

The marinade

> 1 gallon water
> ½ cup coarse sea salt
> 2 large stems crown dill (stems with flowering heads)
> ⅓ cup (2 ounces) packed brown sugar
> 12 ounces porter or dark beer

The crayfish

> 2 gallons water
> ¼ cup sea salt
> 2 bay leaves
> 2 sprigs fresh dill
> 6 whole black peppercorns
> 2 pounds live crayfish

Make the marinade

Bring the water, salt, whole crown dill stems, and brown sugar to a boil in a large pot and simmer for 20 minutes. Cool the marinade to room temperature, then add the porter. Chill the marinade in a large container for several hours.

Cook and marinate the crayfish

Bring the water, salt, bay leaves, dill, and peppercorns to a rolling boil in a large pot. Add the crayfish and cook over high heat until the crayfish bodies turn a uniform red, 3 to 5 minutes.

Remove the crayfish from the water, either by pouring the contents of the pot into a colander or, if the pot is too heavy, by lifting the crayfish from the water with a strainer or a slotted spoon. Add the crayfish to the marinade and refrigerate for at least 12 hours or up to 2 days before serving.

Serve the crayfish

Line a serving platter with dill sprigs. Remove the crayfish from the marinade and arrange them attractively on the platter. Serve with small glasses of very cold aquavit.

CRAYFISH BOIL

The amount of crayfish one person can consume depends on her appetite and other components of the meal. Waverley Root reports a record of thirty-three pounds of crayfish tails downed in two hours at the time his book, *Food*, was published. If your guests eat more moderately, a pound and a half per person should be ample. Serve with crusty bread and either beer or white wine.

So that the water quickly returns to a boil when the crayfish go in, cook them in two pots.

4 SERVINGS
> 6 gallons water
> ½ cup coarse sea salt
> 4 bay leaves
> 2 stalks celery, roughly chopped
> 2 carrots, roughly chopped
> 2 onions, roughly chopped
> 2 handfuls parsley stalks
> 8 whole peppercorns
> 4 small dried chiles
> 6 pounds live crayfish

Divide the water, salt, bay leaves, celery, carrots, onions, parsley stalks, peppercorns, and chiles between two large pots. Bring to a boil, simmer for 10 minutes, and then return to a rolling boil. Put 3 pounds of crayfish into each pot. Cook until they turn red, 3 to 5 minutes.

Drain the crayfish, either by pouring the contents of the pot into a large colander or by lifting them out of the water with a strainer, discarding the seasonings. Pile the crayfish on a large platter and serve.

Lunch at the Bakery

PEOPLE WHO EAT IN RESTAURANTS and who frequent bakeries often think that the chefs and bakers who work in these establishments stuff themselves with delicacies all day long. It's a childhood fantasy come true—an unending supply of favorite foods stacked in walk-in refrigerators waiting to be nibbled. When I had a bakery, I was asked many times how I stayed so thin. "If I worked here, I'd weigh five hundred pounds" was a frequent comment from customers. I always answered that the hard work kept me trim. When I got hungry at the bakery, I wanted "real food," not tarts or chocolate mousse. During the early years of the bakery, I simply wanted slices of bread and cheese. That changed with the passage of time.

We always paced our work so we could stop for a quick lunch. The back room was buzzing: sixteen flourless chocolate cakes baking in the ovens, their intense flavor permeating the room; a batch of tart dough—fifteen pounds of butter, sugar, eggs, almonds, and twenty pounds of flour—amalgamating in the sixty-quart mixer; two hundred pounds of sourdough kneading in the spiral mixer; and two dozen egg whites waiting to be whipped into meringue. We washed the wooden work table, retrieved plates from the stove shelf, and removed cheese from the refrigerator. Someone would ask, "Which bread shall we have today?" It was selected and sliced. Then we sat down on the roll-around flour bins, relieved to be off our feet, and ate with minimal distraction; getting up to answer a phone call or to turn off a mixer. It was more than just a simple meal; it was a time to relax and fortify, read the newspaper, and socialize a bit.

Although we could meet the challenge of making the same pastries and breads repeatedly, eventually we couldn't do the same with the cheese sandwiches we ate every day. We couldn't face one more. So we ordered some vegetables along with the fruit for tarts—crates of the first young asparagus, boxes of tender lettuce mix, broccoli. Our lunches followed the seasons. Sweet white corn was a favorite. In the summer, ears of corn and bread made up the entire lunch for several days on end. We sat at the table and gnawed ear after ear, some going back and forth typewriter fashion, others going around the cobs, dripping corn juice and butter on the plates that we mopped up with chunks of bread.

Months passed. Lunches of quickly cooked vegetables and plentiful fresh bread were satisfying, but our taste buds cried out for more. One of our suppliers made a fortuitous decision. He added pasta to his offerings. My orders changed: "Five cases of bittersweet chocolate, a case of cocoa, and three kilos of pistachio paste, please—oh, and a case of penne." This opened up a whole new world. We needed something that could be assembled quickly, and noodles fit the bill. Cream and saffron moistened some plates. Blue cheese, purchased specifically for lunch use, dressed other bowls.

For a long time, it was principally the bakers who got the pasta on the table. But one day, all of us were too pressed to stop. When Brendan MacRae, a college student who packed and delivered bread to wholesale customers, returned at about noon, I asked, "Brendan, would you start the water for pasta, then slice and sauté some onions? Please? We're starving!" That simple request changed things at the bakery. Brendan boiled water and dropped in a pound of penne. He sliced onions, sautéed them in olive oil, tossed them with the al dente pasta, and showered the pan with grated Asiago cheese. We ate it by the forkful, sitting at the work table. After that day, Brendan started assembling lunch regularly; the pasta with onions and cheese became his signature dish.

Our palates became jaded once again. Pasta went the way of the cheese sandwiches. Boxes of unused fusilli sat beside the onions in the back storeroom. We tried savory bread puddings. Everyone liked them, but they had one drawback—the cooking time was almost an hour. If we thought far enough ahead, someone took a few minutes to make one, using leftover bread and a cheese-egg custard.

Then one day I threw together an asparagus soufflé. It was a welcome change, but like the bread puddings, took a long time to bake. Brendan made the next soufflé, following instructions from me, my hands buried in sticky brioche dough. The following day, he returned from his rounds and, with a sly look on his face, started lunch. He separated eggs, putting the whites in the mixer bowl and setting the yolks aside. Next he melted butter and whisked in flour. Then he whisked in the yolks and some goat cheese. He whipped the whites and folded them into the warm base, poured it all into a buttered soufflé dish, and triumphantly put his master-piece in the oven. Within thirty minutes, its brown top towered two inches above the dish. It deflated slightly when we spooned it onto plates, but the texture remained light and airy, trapping the cheese taste in its web.

Our need for stimulating lunches seemed to mount each fall as the busy holiday season approached. But sometimes carving out time for a simple meal was difficult. The weeks between Halloween and Christmas became a blur, and clear vision didn't return until the first of January.

The day before Thanksgiving was extraordinarily stressful. There was no time to make even the simplest lunch, so I roasted a turkey at home before the holiday week. Then, when I got home on Tuesday night, Sidney helped me assemble a few salads. He carved the turkey, arranged a platter of turkey and the salads, and walked it up the street to the night bread bakers while I went to bed. The next day (at 3:00 A.M. or so), I sleep-walked to the bakery with a platter.

Christmas Eve was another matter. Cooking anything extra was impossible. Tarts filled every oven shelf. The sixty-quart mixer whipped hazelnut buttercream. Vats of melted chocolate were folded into meringue and whipped cream to make mousse for the outsides of countless *bûches de Noël,* being assembled on every available work surface—pipe the mousse from a pastry bag, decorate with meringue mushrooms and candied cran-berries, slide it into the refrigerator, start on another. Bags of bread were crammed in the retail store. A line of customers snaked down the side-walk, waiting to pick up orders. The phone rang incessantly. "Is it too late to place an order?" "Can you save me a loaf of sourdough?" "I'm making a pumpkin cheesecake and I have a question. Is one of the bakers free?" Feeling only slightly guilty, I took both phones off the hook.

One year, a former employee and college student came back to help us through the Christmas season. He had another holiday job on Fisherman's Wharf, a rough and tumble one, befitting the tradition there. At noon on Christmas Eve, he marched into the bakery with a surprise—a large box of cooked crabs. When the last tart was glazed, the last chocolate cake topped with a candied chestnut, and the last *bûche de Noël* dusted with powdered sugar, we cleared the tables and covered them with parchment paper. We piled the crabs in the middle and sliced several loaves of sourdough bread. Then we ate, twisting shells from the leg meat, prying succulent pieces from the bodies with our fingers, savoring every morsel. Silence reigned for the first five minutes as we concentrated on the sweetness of the crab and the tang of the bread. That year started a tradition. On subsequent Christmas Eves, we had Dungeness crabs for lunch, sometimes delivered by a friendly fish purveyor, other years picked up by Sidney or our son, Casey, at a local market. And as with the Thanksgiving turkey, cracked crab was always delivered the evening before to the bread bakers who toiled through the night.

PENNE WITH SAFFRON CREAM SAUCE

This sauce is made in the time it takes to cook the pasta. Saffron, although expensive, goes a long way and will keep, tightly wrapped, for several months. Lightly toasting the saffron brings out its flavor.

Serve small portions of this as a first course, then follow with something light and lean, such as grilled fish, as a counterpoint to the richness of the sauce. Or serve larger portions as a main course.

4 TO 6 SERVINGS

½ teaspoon saffron threads
2 cups (16 ounces) heavy whipping cream
Salt and pepper
1 tablespoon lemon juice
1 tablespoon chopped parsley
1 pound dried penne, preferably Italian

Begin heating a 6-quart pot of generously salted water for the pasta.

Put the saffron threads in a skillet large enough to hold the cream. Over medium heat, toss the saffron threads with your fingers. When the skillet is too hot for your fingers, the saffron should be dry and brittle. Add the cream, a few pinches of salt, and a pinch of pepper, and bring to a gentle boil.

When the pasta water is boiling, add the penne, give it a stir, and return to a boil.

While the pasta is cooking, boil the saffron cream until it is reduced by about a third. It will thicken as it cooks. Stir the lemon juice into the saffron cream when the pasta is almost done.

When the pasta is al dente, drain it and return it to the cooking pot. Bring the sauce back to a boil, tasting for salt and pepper, then pour it over the penne, sprinkle in the parsley, and toss everything together. Serve immediately in hot bowls.

SAVORY BREAD PUDDING

If you have stale bread, don't throw it away; make this instead. Just about any kind of bread will work. Although it takes some time to bake, the preparation time is minimal.

Use whatever herbs you have, balancing mild and assertive together and including either scallions or chives. It's important that the herbs be fresh, not dried. They needn't be exotic—parsley and scallions will suffice if that's all that's available. The cheese can also vary—a bit of a hard grating cheese mixed with a milder one works well.

Many San Francisco restaurants serve bread pudding as an accompaniment to a variety of meat and poultry dishes, often dressed with a touch of the roasting juices.

4 SERVINGS

    8 ounces stale, but not rock-hard bread, torn into 2-inch pieces
    ½ cup finely chopped fresh herbs
    ¾ cup grated cheese
    ¼ cup chopped smoked ham
    3 cups (24 ounces) whole milk
    5 extra-large eggs
    ¾ teaspoon salt
    ¼ teaspoon pepper

Preheat the oven to 350°F.

Butter a 9 x 12-inch gratin dish.

Toss the bread pieces with the herbs, cheese, and ham, then spread in the gratin dish.

Whisk the milk, eggs, salt, and pepper together in a large bowl, and pour this batter over the bread.

Bake the pudding in the middle of the oven until the custard is set and browned, about 45 minutes. Serve hot.

GOAT CHEESE SOUFFLE

Soufflés have a reputation for being difficult to make, but they really aren't. I once gave soufflé-making instructions to my husband over the phone. Overwhipping the egg whites or overfolding the mixture are the most common causes of failure. The whites will beat best when they are truly at room temperature. A soufflé waits for no one. Serve it immediately.

This makes a lovely first course or a light lunch, accompanied by a salad.

4 SERVINGS

4 extra-large eggs at room temperature
1 cup (8 ounces) whole milk
2 tablespoons (1 ounce) butter
3 tablespoons all-purpose flour
4 ounces fresh goat cheese
1 tablespoon snipped chives
White pepper and salt

Preheat the oven to 375°F.

Generously butter an 8-cup soufflé dish.

Separate the eggs. Put the whites in the bowl of a heavy-duty mixer and the yolks in a small bowl.

Heat the milk to a simmer in a small pan. Set aside. In a medium saucepan, melt the butter. Add the flour and whisk constantly over medium heat for 1 minute without letting it color. Add the milk all at once, continuing to whisk. Cook until the mixture just bubbles and thickens, a few minutes. Remove the pan from the heat and let cool for a minute, stirring occasionally. Whisk in the egg yolks, one at a time, then the cheese. Add the chives and 2 pinches of white pepper. Add a pinch of salt, unless the cheese is very salty.

Beat the whites with a whisk attachment, starting at a slow speed until they break up and start to froth, then at a higher speed until soft, droopy peaks form when the whisk is lifted from the bowl. They should still look wet. Fold a dollop of whites into the yolk/cheese mixture, then pour this mixture down the side of the mixing bowl containing the whites. Fold in the rest of the whites. It's better to leave a few clumps of white showing than to overfold.

Pour the mixture into the soufflé dish and place on the middle rack of the oven. Bake until the soufflé has risen above the top of the dish and is browned on top, 30 to 35 minutes. Take to the table immediately and serve on warm plates.

Found Food

A WEEK OF STEADY RAIN had brought out the fruiting fungi the night I attended my first meeting of the Mycological Society of San Francisco. The monthly meetings start at 8:00 P.M., and during the hour beforehand people bring foraged mushrooms for identification. Although I already knew what it was, I had brought a black chanterelle specimen *(Craterellus cornucopioides)* that we had picked outside the front door at our country house.

People trooped in, some of them looking as if they had just emerged from the woods, wearing heavy coats and woolen hats, carrying mushrooms in paper bags or wrapped in newspaper. The gatherers gingerly removed the fungi from their wraps and placed them on the specimen table. Knowledgeable members of the society greeted some specimens like old friends, turning them over in their hands and sniffing them, and remarked on the more interesting species. One man wrote out identifying tags. Before the hour was up, mushrooms covered two large tables. The findings ranged from a large spongelike blob (good to eat, someone said) to tiny disks ¼ inch in diameter attached to a twig. A heady, woodsy aroma wafted from the tables.

I am wary of wild mushrooms. Fungi found in the woods should not be eaten unless they have been positively identified by an expert. There have been serious mushroom poisonings, and at least two deaths, in the San Francisco Bay Area in the last few years. Almost all fatal mushroom poisonings are caused by members of the *Amanita* genus. These mushrooms have distinguishing characteristics, but their age and condition can alter their appearance, making them look more like edible specimens. Immigrants can mistake *Amanita* for look-alikes that grow in their homeland. The symptoms of deadly mushroom poisoning don't appear immediately. By the time the poisoning agent is identified, it can have caused irreparable damage to the liver.

With these thoughts in mind, I didn't share Sidney's enthusiasm when he found some black mushrooms under an oak tree on our country property. I wouldn't let him cook them, even though some friends in the Anderson Valley had reported a bumper crop of black chanterelles that year. Had we been in France, the local pharmacist could have identified them. Instead, we gave them to a mushroom-gathering friend, who said they were black chanterelles, also known by the disquieting name of trumpets of death, and ate them happily. The next season, Sidney found more in the same place. I still wouldn't eat them, and I was adamant that he not eat them either. The third time Sidney gathered the same mushrooms we showed them to the friend who had consumed the first two batches as well as another friend who is an expert. It was only after their affirmation that they were indeed *Craterellus cornucopioides* that I relented. We washed them, chopped them, sautéed them with shallots, and cooked them in a risotto. Their earthy flavor permeated the dish, and even after cooking, they had a nice crunch. That risotto was very good, but the one I ate that fall at Palio d'Asti, a San Francisco restaurant, was even better. It was the height of the Italian white truffle season, and Gianni Fassio, the restaurant's owner, had just returned from a truffle-buying trip in Piedmont. *Risotto con fonduta* was the dish of the day. Waiters carried steaming plates of the cheese-rich rice from the kitchen. Gianni darted around the dining room, shaving thin slices from a large white truffle onto the plates, carrying the truffle and a special cutter wrapped in a napkin and tucked into the pocket of his suit coat between applications. (Imagine the earthy smell of his coat at the end of the day!) The aroma and the taste were intoxicating.

The black chanterelles and that first Mycological Society meeting piqued my interest in mushrooms. I decided to go on one of the society's forays the following Sunday. The designated meeting spot was by the fountain in front of the Palace of the Legion of Honor, a museum on the bluffs above the ocean at the western end of San Francisco. The surrounding area is appropriately called Land's End. It's a spectacular setting. A January mist cloaked the newly refurbished museum; the Golden Gate Bridge, framed by cypress trees, was barely visible in the distance. Sixteen people gathered, dressed warmly against the chill, armed with cameras, baskets, trowels, paper bags, and field guides. We got a few strange looks from the museum-goers. A past president of the Mycological Society led the forage. First he distributed a list of Land's End fungi. I was amazed that it contained 120 names. Not all the mushrooms would be growing, but our leader said that we would stop after we found thirty. We crossed the parking lot and walked along the edge of the golf course. People fanned out and brought back mushrooms. There were gilled mushrooms, boletes, puffballs, coral fungi, polypores, and Ascomycetes. Mushrooms were hidden in the duff, attached to logs, blending in with the grass. Some stood tall; others were only millimeters high. They were inky black, purple, lilac, yellow, orange, brown, and white. Some smelled like anise, others like the earth. They had fanciful common names such as dung dome, witch's hat, shaggy mane, and plums and custard. One made a tasty soup when fresh, another tasted like cardboard when cooked (several people insisted), and others were poisonous. I looked, smelled, and struggled to catch the botanical names. We had found twenty species within a few feet of the parking lot.

We skirted the edge of the golf course, striding faster when we heard someone yell, "Fore!" and followed a meandering path along the cliffs overlooking the ocean. More specimens went into the leader's basket. One man was disappointed that an edible species he found was old and crumbled. The path circumnavigated the golf course and led us back to the parking lot. The group dispersed and I headed for my car, my head swimming with Latin names and images of mushrooms. I was humbled by the mushrooms—their vast numbers, their complex relationships with the trees, how closely they resemble one another. I had respect for the people who have mastered the mushrooms; I had a lot to learn.

Twenty years ago there were no fresh wild mushrooms in grocery stores in the Bay Area, and consumption of all types of mushrooms was half what it is today. Now there are more available; commercial growers produce more per square foot, and mushrooms once considered exotic are now cultivated. The Asian population in the Bay Area, whose cuisine showcases mushrooms, has made them more common in markets and restaurants. And many people are eating less meat—grilled portobellos have replaced steak in many sandwiches.

But these influences hadn't made mushrooms as popular as they are today when Ken Ottoboni was working at a French restaurant in San Francisco in the late 1970s. Then, chefs often purchased wild mushrooms at the back door from a knowledgeable forager. Mushrooms had fascinated Ken since his boyhood days in Monterey, when he looked for porcini with his grandfather, and he realized that there was a potential market for selling gathered mushrooms.

He decided to turn his passion for mushrooms into a business and left his job. He assembled a small crew, and they combed the woods for mushrooms. Soon he didn't go into the woods anymore; his time was spent packing fungi and calling potential buyers. Today, he has two partners who manage the day-to-day business and five buyers who work exclusively for his company. They primarily sell chanterelles but also carry black chanterelles, hedgehogs, porcini, and morels.

Much has changed since the early days, when no one would buy black chanterelles, forcing Ken to ship them to Europe for a low price. Now his company sells 200,000 pounds of mushrooms in a good year. (This is considered a small- to medium-size company.) His buyers travel all over the western states and trade with freelance gatherers. The secret places of fifteen years ago are now public knowledge, and the competition is fierce. Mother Nature holds the upper hand; the harvests are unpredictable. Ken misses the foraging days when his company was young. He still spends his free time tromping through the woods, eyes scanning the ground.

People have tried to cultivate chanterelles, with limited success. One stumbling block is the symbiotic relationship, known as mycorrhizal, that these mushrooms have with the roots of the trees where they grow.

Truffles, the black (French) and white (Italian) diamonds that grow underground, are even more elusive. I found a text published in 1906 in France that described planting trees for truffle production. (The book was a treasure—the spine was weakened and the cover faded, the uneven-sized pages aged to a dark brown at their edges.) Either acorns or young trees were recommended. After two years of growth, farmers inoculated the new trees by scattering soil from a producing truffle orchard around their bases. The success rate wasn't mentioned, but the tone of the book was optimistic, as if failure wasn't a possibility. There have been more recent attempts to cultivate truffles in Texas and California. I talked to a man who is a partner in a truffle farm hidden down miles of dirt road in Mendocino County. They planted hazelnut trees inoculated with the truffle fungus in 1982 and boast of heavy crops that others in California haven't been able to replicate. When I asked him the reason for their success, he said, "It's something special that we do to the trees every year. But you could videotape it and still wouldn't know." That's all he would reveal. Garland Gourmet in Hillsborough, North Carolina, claims to be the first commercially successful truffle grower in the Western Hemisphere. They harvested their first truffles in 1993, thirteen years after planting inoculated trees. They sell both truffles and trees.

The information about the truffle trees intrigued me. I started to speculate. If we planted a seeded tree on our country property, we could be harvesting truffles in a decade. Their exorbitant price wouldn't matter anymore. I thought of a fresh black truffle that we had sliced and slipped under the skin of a Thanksgiving turkey breast years ago. If we had our own supply, we could stuff the cavity of the bird with them as well. We could stud a *foie gras* terrine with them. And if we were really feeling decadent, we could add a whole, sliced truffle to scrambled eggs for breakfast. Assuming the tree produced. A big assumption, said Sidney.

Wild mushrooms aren't the only interesting edible mushrooms. There are also delicious cultivated mushrooms; not all of them are the ubiquitous white mushrooms found in every supermarket. John and Toby Garrone of Hazel Dell Mushroom Farms had a space across from my bakery's stall at the Ferry Plaza Farmers' Market. They still sell mushrooms at that market, as well as at several others in the Bay Area. Other vendors display their wares on tables in the open air, or under tall umbrellas. The Garrones' mushroom stall looks like a cave, enclosed with tarpaulins, the roof jutting out to protect the fungi from the elements. The mushrooms probably feel very much at home. (Old quarry caves near Paris were used for decades to cultivate mushrooms.) In addition to the common white and brown mushrooms, the Garrones sell portobello, shiitake, and oyster mushrooms. They grow them on sterile blocks of sawdust and rice bran that have been impregnated with mycelium, the fungal matrix that eventually fruits to produce mushrooms.

Home mushroom kits that use these same blocks are available. One Christmas, I gave a shiitake kit to Sidney and a portobello one to our son, Casey. Within a month, Casey reported that mushrooms were starting to appear. Sidney's started out as a mottled block that we watered regularly and kept covered with plastic. Slowly one of the brown specks grew into a mushroom. We sautéed it and ate it standing in the kitchen. Eventually more brown spots developed fruit, and in a span of two months we harvested six or seven shiitakes. It seems like an arduous way of getting mushrooms, but if we need a lot, I know the Garrones' market schedule. And when they're in season, I know where to get black chanterelles.

Mushroom Appetizer Puffs

These are made exactly like *gougères,* cream puffs with cheese mixed into the paste, except that sautéed mushrooms are substituted for the cheese. Use mushrooms with a pronounced flavor, such as shiitakes or chanterelles. I thank Larry Stickney of the San Francisco Mycological Society for giving me this idea.

The puffs are best the day they are made. Crisp them in a 375°F oven if you keep them overnight.

ABOUT 36 PUFFS, 6 APPETIZER SERVINGS

The mushrooms

> *5 ounces raw shiitake or chanterelle mushrooms*
> *2 tablespoons (1 ounce) unsalted butter*
> *Salt and pepper*

The cream puff paste

> *½ cup (4 ounces) whole milk*
> *½ cup (4 ounces) water*
> *1 teaspoon salt*
> *6 tablespoons (3 ounces) unsalted butter*
> *1 cup (5 ounces) unbleached all-purpose flour*
> *4 extra-large eggs*

Sauté the mushrooms

Clean the mushrooms with a damp towel or a soft brush. Chop them into a fine dice. Heat the butter in a 12-inch skillet. Add the mushrooms and sauté them over high heat, stirring frequently, until they give off their liquid and soften, about 5 minutes. They will still be a little toothsome. Add salt and pepper to taste and set aside.

Make the puffs

Preheat the oven to 375°F.

Place the milk, water, salt, and butter in a medium saucepan. Heat the mixture until the butter is melted and the mixture starts to boil. Remove from the heat. Add the flour all at once and stir vigorously with a wooden spoon. Return to the heat and cook the paste for another minute, stirring continuously. Transfer the mass to the bowl of a heavy-duty mixer fitted with the paddle. With the machine on medium speed, add the eggs, one at a time, waiting until each one is incorporated before adding the next. Add the reserved mushrooms.

Line a baking sheet with parchment paper. Fill a pastry bag with the mixture. Don't use a tip; the mushrooms may clog it. Pipe the puff paste into mounds, 1½ inches in diameter, 1 inch apart. If you aren't adept with a pastry bag, drop the mixture onto the baking sheet from a tablespoon.

Bake them in the middle of the oven until they puff and brown, about 20 minutes. They should feel firm to the touch. Let them cool, then serve with cocktails or wine before dinner.

RISOTTO WITH BLACK CHANTERELLES

Roasting the fresh mushrooms is a good way to evaporate their moisture and make them firmer before adding them to the risotto.

Use a good-quality cheese; it really makes a difference in this dish.

4 SERVINGS

> ½ pound fresh black chanterelles
> 4 to 5 cups chicken stock
> 3 tablespoons (1½ ounces) butter
> 2 shallots, finely chopped (about ¼ cup)
> 1½ cups Arborio rice
> Salt to taste
> ⅔ cup grated Parmigiano-Reggiano or grana cheese

Preheat the oven to 500°F.

Wash the mushrooms carefully. Cut off the bottoms so that the water can flow freely through their trumpet shape. Dry them carefully on paper towels until no visible moisture remains. Place them in a single layer on a parchment-lined baking sheet and roast them in the oven until their moisture is gone and they look slightly shriveled, about 5 minutes. Set aside.

Bring the chicken stock to a simmer and turn the heat to low to keep it hot.

Melt the butter in a medium saucepan. Add the shallots and rice, and stir until the mixture is well coated with butter and glistening, 2 to 3 minutes. Add about 1 cup of the hot stock. Over medium-low heat, cook the rice until most of the liquid is absorbed, stirring constantly. Continue adding stock as it becomes absorbed. The rice will swell and become creamy as it cooks. Add salt to taste. (The amount will depend on the saltiness of the stock.) After 15 minutes of cooking, add the mushrooms. Cook until the rice is slightly al dente, timing the addition of liquid so that the mixture is creamy, not soupy, when the rice is finished. Stir in the cheese at the end.

Serve immediately in warm bowls.

ROAST CHICKEN WITH MUSHROOMS

Because black truffles are so rare and costly, cooks have devised ways to extend their flavor. Embedding a single fresh truffle in a large jar of rice for a few days will perfume every grain of rice with truffle essence. Slipping thin slices of truffle under the skin of a chicken or turkey before roasting will infuse the whole bird.

Lacking fresh truffles, you can still impart a mushroom taste to a chicken, as this dish shows. Wild chanterelles or cultivated shiitakes are a good choice. The common white button mushrooms aren't flavorful enough.

Start the meal with roasted beets, slipped from their skins and dressed with vinaigrette, then serve roasted potatoes with the chicken.

4 SERVINGS

½ pound fresh chanterelle or shiitake mushrooms
2 cloves garlic
2 scallions
2 tablespoons finely chopped parsley
3 tablespoons (1½ ounces) olive oil
Salt and pepper
1 (4 pound) roasting chicken
1 stalk celery
1 carrot
Few sprigs parsley
Salt and pepper
1 cup (8 ounces) chicken stock

Prepare the mushrooms

Clean the mushrooms with a damp towel or a soft brush. Chop them into a fine dice. Finely dice the garlic and scallions. Heat the olive oil in a 12-inch skillet. Add the mushrooms, garlic, and scallions and cook over high heat, stirring frequently, until the mushrooms give off their liquid and are glistening with the oil and the garlic and scallions are lightly browned. Stir in the chopped parsley. Add salt and pepper to taste. Set the cooked mushrooms aside and let them cool to room temperature.

Roast the chicken

Preheat the oven to 375°F.

Wash the chicken inside and out and pat dry with paper towels. Using your fingers, carefully separate the skin over the breast from the flesh, starting at the cavity end. Also separate the skin from each thigh and drumstick. Go slowly, being careful not to tear the skin.

Distribute the mushroom mixture under the loosened skin. Put the celery stalk, carrot, and parsley sprigs in the cavity and truss the chicken. Sprinkle the bird with salt and pepper.

Place the chicken in a roasting pan, breast side up. Roast, basting occasionally with the pan juices, until the skin is browned and an instant-read thermometer reads 180°F when plunged into the crease between the body and the thigh, about 1 hour, 20 minutes.

Remove the chicken to a cutting board. Pour most of the fat from the roasting pan. Add the chicken stock. Bring the stock to a boil, scraping any browned pieces from the bottom of the pan. Season with salt and pepper. Pour the juice through a strainer into a serving pitcher. Keep it warm (put it in the turned-off oven with the door ajar) while you carve the chicken and place the pieces on a warmed serving platter. Serve the chicken immediately, passing the juice on the side.

Choice Tools

WELL-EQUIPPED KITCHENS DON'T ALL CONTAIN THE SAME THINGS. The tools and appliances reflect the cooking styles and personalities of the owners. A French friend always makes mayonnaise in a bowl with a whisk or, if the mayonnaise is aioli, with a mortar and pestle. It's the way her family did it when she was growing up. Sidney is the mayonnaise maker in our house, and he often makes it in a food processor. No one made mayonnaise during his childhood years—it came out of a jar.

Sidney and I brought rudimentary cooking skills to our marriage, with utensils to match. As we became better cooks, our *batterie de cuisine* expanded. Two years after we were married, we spent a month traversing the French countryside. We stumbled upon Villedieu-les-Poêles, a small town in Normandy, where the major occupation was making copper pots. We knew that copper cookware conducted heat better than anything else, and we had priced some pots at home. The ones in this small village were bargains. We chose five saucepans that nestled inside one another and bought lids to match. We lugged them around, strapped to the back of our motorcycle, for the rest of the trip. Almost thirty years later, we still use them daily. We've gradually added more to our collection—casseroles of various sizes and a few large skillets. The only drawback is their tin lining, which melts if the pan is heated without liquid or if the cooking liquid evaporates. A few suffered the consequences of our teenagers' cooking, plus a few mistakes of our own, but fortunately there's a local company that re-tins them.

Shortly after we moved to San Francisco, someone in a cooking class I attended talked about buying small kitchen appliances from secondhand stores at rock-bottom prices. We frequented such stores, looking for furnishings for our sparse flat, so we added the appliance sections during our excursions. One Sunday afternoon, after a disappointing tour of the Purple Heart Thrift Shop, we headed for the door. In a far corner, near the front, Sidney spied a locked cage containing electrical equipment. Buried in one corner was an old Kitchen-Aid mixer, larger than a home model, with a chrome finish. We strained to read the price tag. Could it be right? It said $10.95. None of the employees had a key, only the manager, who wasn't there. We couldn't come back until the next weekend and were afraid that it might be gone by then. One of the employees rummaged through the office and found a large ring of keys. The first two didn't work. He tried another. It fit—the lock slipped open. When we hauled out the mixer, we discovered a new problem. It didn't have a plug. We couldn't try it out. "I can't guarantee that it works," said the salesperson. For a moment, I thought that Sidney was going to have the audacity to ask for a lower price (he *is* from New York), but he looked at me with a straight face and said, "What do you think; shall we take a chance?" "Let's buy it," I said. Then we saw a cardboard box full of attachments. "These don't have a separate price tag, so I guess they just go with the mixer," said the salesperson. The box held the usual things— a bowl, a whisk, a paddle, and a dough hook, but also contained a meat grinder, a cheese grater, two screens and an attachment with heavy porcelain rollers for making purées, and another gadget that I still haven't figured out. We paid for our prize and tried to control our giddiness as we left the store, but we were doubled over with laughter by the time we got to the car. Fitted with a new plug, the mixer actually ran, but we took it to the Kitchen-Aid distributor for a tune-up. The man who fixed it said it was from the 1930s and, judging from the crumbs inside, thought it came from a bakery. That mixer was a fortune-teller. Fifteen years later, when I took it to my bakery, I bought a newer model for Sidney one Christmas. Now, with the bakery closed, the old one stays at our country home, kneading bread dough, whipping egg whites, and mixing cake batters. If I could buy only one major kitchen appliance, it would be a heavy-duty mixer.

Since I love to bake, I have other accoutrements to help me besides my mixer. But the ones I turn to the most are the simplest ones—a sturdy rolling pin, straight without handles, tin tart pans with removable bottoms, various cake pans, baking sheets from a restaurant supply store, tiles I bought at a masonry store for my oven when I bake bread, a peel, and a scale. Actually, I have three scales: two left over from the bakery and one that hangs on the wall with a bottom that folds up. Using a scale, especially to bake, is so much more logical and accurate. I wish I could convince everyone to buy one. I also wish I could convert everyone to the metric system, but that prospect seems dimmer than persuading people to use a scale.

One of the homeliest things we own is a large aluminum pot with an insert to hold pasta and another for steaming. It's more than twenty years old. The sides are dented from hitting the ceramic tile floor, and the blackened bottom could use a good scrubbing. We've probably cooked hundreds of pounds of pasta in it and steamed as many pounds of vegetables. I can't imagine our kitchen without it. Nor would I ever give up my salad spinner, purchased in Brussels in 1976.

I am hopeless about sharpening knives, including the ones we bought at the Henckels factory store in Solingen, Germany. We were living in Brussels and drove to Solingen on Armistice Day, celebrated by the Belgians but obviously not by the Germans. The knives at the store were fine-quality specimens, and we had a hard time choosing a set. Finally, we settled on four chef's knives of varying sizes, a paring knife, a bread knife, a sharpening steel, and a carving knife and fork. Over the years we have added filleting and boning knives and a few more paring knives. Sidney keeps them sharp, with a steel and sometimes with a stone. When they need professional help, we take them to the knife sharpener at the Ferry Plaza Farmers' Market. Although we have quite a collection, the knives I reach for most are the six-inch and eight-inch chef's knives and the paring knife. These favorites influenced my selection when I bought cutlery for the bakery, but longer chef's knives were better suited for the volume of chopping.

Because I'm comfortable chopping, mincing, and dicing with my knives, I resisted getting a food processor for a long time. When I wanted thin slices or julienne shapes, I used my French mandoline. A sale of Cuisinarts convinced me to try one. I like their puréeing and emulsifying capabilities, but I still don't use the processor for chopping unless the quantity is very large.

It's easy to be tempted by every new kitchen gadget that comes along, but many are superfluous. People should choose equipment that entices them into the kitchen and helps them cook. I guess for some that might even include a microwave and a bread machine.

MY FRIEND JEROME

WHEN I THINK OF MY FRIEND JEROME, three disparate things pop into my mind—hair, plums, and tamales. My hairdresser and food-loving friend grew up in a Mexican-American family and has a plum tree that is worthy of a botanical study. Despite benign neglect and haphazard pruning, it produces a prodigious amount of fruit every year—small plums with almost purple skin and cherry-colored flesh. Since he inherited the tree when he bought the house, Jerome doesn't know what species it is, maybe a cross of Santa Rosa and something else. I first became acquainted with Jerome's plums one August afternoon when his car stopped in front of the bakery. I saw him more often at his salon when he cut my hair than at the bakery, so his arrival was a pleasant surprise. He opened the trunk of the car, lifted out a large box, and pushed open the screen door. It was full of very ripe plums. He set the box on a table with a thud and went back to the car for another. "Fran, I have so many plums this year, I don't know what to do. You can use these, can't you?" he asked. The two boxes of oozing fruit were far more than we could use for tarts, so we made preserves out of most of them.

That was the first of many shipments of plums from Jerome. He often arrived just as the day crew was about to leave. "Here comes Jerome—and he has plums," one of the bakers would say, a dismayed look on her face. It's not that she didn't like the fruit, but she knew that it was very ripe and we would have to do something with it quickly. So we devised new recipes. In addition to tarts, clafoutis, and preserves, we puréed cooked plums and filled baked tart shells with the intense paste, then decorated the top with halved raw plums. The purée still had the plums' tart taste, and its dense texture contrasted with the juicy fruit on top. We packed plums into three-quart jars, covered them with vodka and a little sugar, then put them on a shelf in the office for three months while the alcohol permeated and preserved them. In the winter, when fresh plums were long gone, we drained them and baked them into "sugar-plum" cakes. They made fine gifts, dusted with powdered sugar, wrapped in cellophane, and tied with a bow. But the preserves made from this fruit were so superior to those made from other plums that they became famous, and people would ask specifically for Jerome's plum preserves.

Sometimes when Jerome didn't have time to bring us the plums, the delivery driver would pick them up at his salon. One year, when Jerome was too busy to even pick the fruit, I went to his garden one hot July day. He held a ladder against the tall tree while I climbed into the leaves and filled plastic sacks dangling from the top of the ladder. Jerome shouted directions: "Over to the left, behind you, there's a big cluster. Go up one more rung and you can reach a lot more." That year I hauled a record quantity to the bakery.

Jerome Castillo grew up in a Mexican-American family in Benicia, a small town on the Sacramento River an hour east of San Francisco. But the community was Portuguese-American, so he was exposed to that culinary influence too. Later, he lived in Guam, where the nuances of Pacific Island ingredients and preparation crept into his kitchen. He has a keen appreciation of food and loves to cook. We always talk about food as he cuts my hair. "Fran, have you been to any new restaurants?" Snip, snip. "We baked the best fish last night. Halibut, with sliced fresh red onion and tomatoes, salt and pepper, served with the cooking juices poured over it. Delicious," as he stopped cutting long enough to kiss the tips of his fingers. He has also given me new ideas. When he saw the *fraises des bois* in my country garden, he suggested tossing a few in green salads. It's a perfect combination, tiny bursts of sweetness mingled with the crunchy greens.

Jerome seems to attract food lovers for clients. I'm not the only one discussing the intricacies of puff pastry or the best stuffing for chicken sausages while I'm being coiffed. Chefs, both retired and running kitchens, and food writers rotate through his chair, all discussing new ideas or relating their favorite recipes, which Jerome hurries home to try.

We should all meet at the salon for lunch some day.

Once, while working on my hair, Jerome described a recipe for tamales. He frequently gathered family and friends near Christmas for tamale making—marathon sessions that produced at least a hundred filled corn husks. I was always too busy baking to even consider participating.

The tamales Jerome described sounded more intriguing than the ubiquitous beans and rice found at the tacquerias that line San Francisco's Mission Street. And I liked the notion of families gathering to make something special for the holidays. So that summer I coaxed him to show me the preparation. He has changed the original recipe over the years, adding his own twists, so he invited his sister and brother-in-law to the tamale day. "He's the expert," said Jerome.

I drove to his house on a warm Sunday in June. The kitchen doors were open to the deck, where the roses peeked over the railing. Mike Diaz (the expert) and his wife, Angie, had not arrived, so Jerome showed me how he made masa, a dough consisting of a type of large-kernel field corn that has been treated with lime and then ground. He had just started assembling ingredients when he suddenly stopped. "I forgot one important thing," he said, running to the next room. Within seconds, Mexican music filled the air. Instead of soaking and grinding the special corn himself, Jerome used Quaker masa harina, a flour made by drying fresh masa. He measured the masa harina and put it in a bowl. Then he added warmed milk and coconut milk and mixed it with his hands, making a dry dough. Next he beat butter in a mixer bowl with salt and baking powder. He added the dough to the butter, then a cup of corn kernels. He continued to mix with his hands, adding a bit more milk until the consistency seemed right.

Snarled traffic delayed Mike and Angie's arrival. They needed help carrying supplies from their van—large boxes holding ten pounds of fresh masa purchased from a Mexican store, plus a bag of masa harina, ten pounds of pork loin they had cooked the previous day, a huge jar of red chile sauce, various spices, and dried corn husks. Another cardboard box held a twenty-quart pot and the "stackers," three pots with perforated bottoms that fit on top of one another and that would hold the tamales as they steamed. "We'll just make a small batch today," said Mike. "Usually we start with thirty pounds of masa."

Mike was all business. He took off his shirt and tied an apron over his T-shirt, never touching the golf hat on his head. Jerome's wife, Annette, Angie, and I separated corn husks and put them in a large pot to soak in boiling water. This softens them and makes them pliable enough to stuff. Mike put the ten pounds of fresh masa in a big stainless bowl. He had persuaded the store to make a special batch, as they usually only make it near Christmas. Jerome remembers his father soaking dried corn in a lime bath for hours, then it was his task to remove the skins and put the kernels through a meat grinder to make the masa. As he got older, Jerome tired of the laborious process and fled the house on tamale-making day. But Mike learned his father-in-law's recipe, and he is the one to carry on the family tradition.

To the fresh masa, Mike added masa harina, baking powder, pork cooking broth, and melted margarine, mixing it carefully with his hands until it looked right. Then he covered the bowl with a damp cloth. There was a discussion about how to protect the glass-topped table. Jerome voted for newspapers. His sister disagreed. Annette suggested an old table-cloth. Mike said, "Let's just work on the table. We can clean up any smeared masa or drops of sauce." An assembly line began. Annette and I removed the corn husks from the hot water, carefully pulled them apart, and discarded any corn silk that was clinging to them. Then we dried them. Using a special spatula from the Mexican food store, Mike applied a thin coat of masa to one side of the large husks, leaving borders all the way around. As I began to help him, he noted, "The masa layer should be very thin. The tamales you get in restaurants always have too much in them." We handed the masa-coated husks to Angie. She put some shredded cooked pork on the masa, a black olive, and a dollop of red chile sauce. Next she folded the edges of the husk together, enclosing the filling. She folded up the bottom and wrapped each tamale in heavy parchment paper. Then she stacked them horizontally in the steamers.

We picked up the pace. As the traditional tamales steamed, Jerome cooked chicken and an accompanying sauce to fill his version. He cut huge frozen banana leaves into pieces and washed them. Then he heated the leaves over a stove burner to soften them. We put a layer of masa on each, leaving borders around the edges. The poached chicken went on top, then some roasted peppers. We folded the long sides together and tied the ends with small strips of leaves. They were ready for steaming.

More tamale eaters arrived—Sidney, as well as Annette's sister and her husband. Mike started another batch of sauce, to show me how it was done. He stood over a large casserole, adding ingredients, tasting, and patiently stirring the entire time. The process took thirty minutes. Halfway through, he added a secret ingredient—ground dried chiles grown in New Mexico by a friend. He assured me that similar New Mexico peppers could be found in Mexican stores. He tasted it carefully, swallowing a spoonful, then thinking. "Taste it," he said. It was very thick, with a sweet heat that rose from my throat after I swallowed.

Although we had made about fifty traditional tamales, a substantial amount of masa remained. "Let's make sweet tamales from the rest," said Angie. She added pieces of apple, cinnamon, brown sugar, raisins, and walnuts, mixing all together, then spreading the mixture on corn husks, which were folded and steamed.

We sat at a round table under a live oak tree beyond the deck and ate the savory tamales moistened with sauce, accompanied by rice and a green salad. All were delicious. Then we sampled the apple-filled version, which reminded me of rice pudding but with a thicker texture. The only thing missing was a tart made from Jerome's plums, but they were still green on the tree.

CALIFORNIA-STYLE PORK TAMALES

After a day of tamale making at my friend's house, I was confused. Jerome and his brother-in-law Mike called their tamale sauce mole. I thought that mole always contained ground nuts and usually some chocolate. And as a baker, I felt that the amount of baking powder in the masa recipes was too high. A little sleuthing answered both questions. Jacqueline Higuera McMahan's book, *California Rancho Cooking*, has a recipe for tamales that is very similar to Mike Diaz's. They have been made by the author's family for more than a hundred years. There is no mole; the sauce is a chile sauce like the one Mike's father-in-law handed down to him. I also discovered that beating air into the masa lightens it, allowing for a smaller amount of baking powder. California chiles, New Mexico chile powder, rendered lard, masa harina, and corn husks are available in Mexican food stores. I use a two-tiered Chinese bamboo steamer set in a skillet to cook the tamales.

The pork and chile sauce can be prepared ahead.

This is my version of Mike Diaz's recipe. I have omitted the traditional canned California black olives and have used lard instead of margarine. Although this amount will make about 20 tamales, if you triple the recipe and invite a few helpers, there will be enough for dinner and extra for everyone to take home. And you'll have more fun.

18 TO 20 TAMALES, 8 SERVINGS

The pork filling
> 2½ pounds. boneless pork butt
> 1 onion, sliced
> 2 cloves garlic, sliced
> ½ teaspoon dried oregano
> 1 teaspoon salt

The chile sauce

8 large dried California chiles (about 3 ounces)
2 tablespoons vegetable oil
2 cloves garlic, finely chopped
2 tablespoons unbleached all-purpose flour
1¼ teaspoons ground cumin
½ teaspoon dried oregano
½ teaspoon salt
1 cup cooking liquid from the pork, warmed
New Mexico chile powder to taste

The corn husks and masa

8 ounces dried corn husks
2 cups (8½ ounces) masa harina
1⅓ cups (10½ ounces) warm water
½ cup (4 ounces) rendered lard or butter at room temperature
1 teaspoon salt
1 teaspoon baking powder
¾ cup cooking liquid from the pork, warmed

Cook the pork

Put the pork, onion, garlic, oregano, and salt in a large pot. Add enough water to barely cover the meat. Bring to a simmer, cover, and cook over low heat until tender, about 2 hours. Cool in the broth. When the meat is cool enough to handle, shred it by hand. Reserve the cooking liquid. This can be made a few days ahead and refrigerated.

Make the chile sauce

Cut the tops off the chiles and discard the seeds. Place the chiles in a large bowl and cover with boiling water. Soak for 45 minutes. Put half of the chiles in a food processor with 1 cup of the soaking water. Process until they are smooth. Pour the purée into a strainer set over a bowl, then purée the rest of the chiles with 1 cup soaking water. Add this batch of purée to the strainer. Push the purée through the strainer with the bottom of a ladle, discarding the skins that remain. There will be about 1⅔ cups.

Heat the oil in a saucepan. Add the garlic and cook until it is soft but not browned. Whisk in the flour and cook until the mixture bubbles. Whisk in the cumin, oregano, and salt. Add the pork cooking liquid and bring it to a boil. Add the chile purée. Simmer, whisking frequently, for 15 minutes, until the sauce has thickened. Taste for seasoning. If you want it a little hotter, add New Mexico chile powder, a little at a time, cooking a few minutes after each addition.

Soak the corn husks and make the masa

Put the corn husks in a large bowl and cover them with hot tap water. Weigh them down with a casserole lid.

Mix the masa harina with the water in a bowl. Knead by hand for a minute until a soft dough is formed. Cover the bowl with plastic wrap and let the dough rest for 30 minutes.

Beat the lard (or butter) with the paddle in the bowl of a heavy-duty mixer until creamy, about 2 minutes. With the mixer running, add the dough in 5 portions, beating well after each addition. Stir the salt and baking powder into the pork cooking liquid. With the mixer running, drizzle the liquid into the bowl. Beat the masa at medium speed until a teaspoon of it will float when placed in a bowl of cold water, about 10 minutes. (The time will be shorter if you use butter instead of lard.) Cover the bowl with plastic wrap until needed.

Assemble and steam the tamales

Take the corn husks out of the water. Separate them, removing any corn silk, and pat dry with kitchen towels. Have the shredded pork and chile sauce at hand. Use the larger husks. Spread a thin layer of masa on the inside (the smooth side) of a husk, leaving a 1-inch border at the sides and 2 inches at top and bottom. Put a few pieces of pork on the dough and a tablespoon of chile sauce on the meat. Fold the sides together so that the masa covers the filling. Fold up the bottom (the narrow end), then fold down the top. Lay the tamale in a basket of a two-tiered steamer, folded ends down. Assemble the rest of the tamales. Place half of them in the bottom steamer and the rest in the top steamer. Steam the tamales over simmering water for 1 hour, checking the water level occasionally. When cool enough to handle, pile the tamales on a serving plate and serve. Heat the rest of the chile sauce and serve it on the side.

JEROME'S TAMALES

Influenced by living in Guam and sparked by his culinary imagination, Jerome devised this version of tamales. The corn he used was one of the new sweet hybrids, which added a new dimension to the masa.

Banana leaves are imported from the Philippines and can be found in the frozen food section of Asian or Mexican food stores. If they are impossible to find, use traditional corn husks.

The filling can be made a day ahead.

18 TO 20 TAMALES, 8 SERVINGS

The chicken filling
1 tablespoon olive oil
¼ teaspoon ground allspice
1 tablespoon chili powder
2 cloves garlic, minced
5½ cups chicken stock
2 whole chicken breasts (4 halves), about 2 pounds
1 teaspoon salt (2 teaspoons if stock is unsalted)

The masa
2 cups (8½ ounces) masa harina
⅔ cup (5 ounces) whole milk
⅔ cup (5 ounces) coconut milk
10 tablespoons (5 ounces) unsalted butter at room temperature
1½ teaspoons salt
1 teaspoon baking powder
2 cups raw corn kernels cut from 4 ears of corn

The peppers and banana leaves
6 medium Anaheim chile peppers
1 pound frozen banana leaves

Make the chicken filling

Heat the olive oil in a large pot. Add the spices and garlic to the oil and cook until fragrant, less than a minute. Add the stock and chicken breasts. Cover, bring to a simmer, and poach until the chicken is just done, about 20 minutes. Remove the chicken and boil until the stock is reduced by half. When the chicken is cool enough to handle, remove the skin and bones and shred the meat by hand. Set the stock and meat aside. This can be made a day ahead and refrigerated.

Make the masa

Mix the masa harina with the milk and coconut milk in a bowl. Knead it by hand for a minute until a soft dough is formed. Cover the bowl with plastic wrap and let the dough rest for 30 minutes.

Place the butter, salt, and baking powder in the bowl of a heavy-duty mixer and beat with the paddle until creamy, about 2 minutes. With the mixer running, add the dough in 5 portions, beating well after each addition. Add the corn kernels. Beat at medium speed until a teaspoon of masa will float when placed in a bowl of cold water, about 8 minutes. Cover the bowl with plastic wrap while you prepare the peppers and banana leaves.

Prepare the peppers and banana leaves

Roast the peppers over a gas stove burner (or under a broiler), turning them as necessary until they are completely charred. Put them in a paper bag until they are cool enough to handle. Rub off the skin under running water. Discard the stems, inside ribs, and seeds. Slice the peppers and set them aside.

Remove the frozen banana leaves from their wrapper. Gently pull them apart and cut them into 10-inch sections across the grain. Trim each piece so that it is 8 inches from top to bottom. Wash and dry the leaves, then heat them briefly over a stove burner to make them more pliable.

Assembled and steam the tamales

Spread a thin layer of the masa dough in the middle of a banana leaf, leaving a 2-inch margin on the long edges and 3 inches at the top and bottom. Put a few pieces of chicken and some peppers in the middle of the masa. Moisten the filling with a tablespoon of the reduced chicken cooking liquid. Fold over the edge nearest you so that the edges of the masa meet. Fold the edges of the leaf together twice to join them together. Fold the ends toward the center. Put the package in a basket of a two-tiered steamer, folded ends down. Assemble the rest of the tamales. Place half of them in the bottom steamer and the rest in the top steamer. Steam the tamales over simmering water for 40 minutes, checking the water level occasionally. When cool enough to handle, pile the tamales on a platter and serve. Heat the rest of the reduced chicken cooking liquid and serve it on the side.

PLUM PRESERVES

We made hundreds of jars of preserves at the bakery from the plums my friend Jerome gave me. His plums made the best preserves, tart and flavorful. One customer bought the preserves by the case, and was always disappointed when we ran out. Use any variety of plums when you make this, but be certain that they are ripe.

The actual cooking takes place after 24 hours of macerating, so start a day before you want to make the preserves. The sugar draws liquid from the plums, and that is cooked first, before the plums are added. This method maintains the integrity of the fruit by minimizing its cooking time.

The proportion of 3 parts fruit to 2 parts sugar by weight can be used if you have a different quantity of fruit than the amount specified below. The same formula can be used for other fruits as well.

SIX PINTS

> *6 pounds 9½ ounces pitted ripe plums (buy an extra pound so that the net weight without the pits will be correct)*
> *4 pounds 6½ ounces granulated sugar (about 11 cups)*
> ***Canning tools:*** *a scale, 6 pint jars with two-part lids, a large pot that will hold all the jars, a noncorroding 8-quart pot (or a copper canning kettle), a candy thermometer, a long-handled slotted spoon for skimming foam, a jar lifter, a ladle, and a widemouthed funnel*

Prepare the fruit

Wash the plums. The pits must be removed from the fruit, but they don't come out easily. One way is to cut the plum around the "seam," going through to the pit and then twisting off one half. Cut the other half off the pit, then cut the fruit into quarters, or into wedges if the plums are large. Weigh the plums after pitting.

Using a stainless steel bowl or a plastic container that will fit into your refrigerator, layer the plums with the sugar, starting with plums and ending with sugar. Cover the bowl and refrigerate for 24 hours, or up to 3 days.

Cook and process the preserves

Place a kitchen towel or a wire rack in the bottom of a large pot. Put 6 clean pint jars into the pot, cover with water, and bring to a boil. Boil for 20 minutes, then turn down the heat, leaving the jars in the hot water. Proceed with the recipe while the jars boil.

Pour the fruit into a large sieve or colander set into a heavy, non-corroding 8-quart pot. Use a copper canning kettle if you have one. When the plums have drained, set them aside. Scrape any undissolved sugar from the macerating container into the pot, and give the syrup a stir so that any undissolved sugar won't stick during the beginning stage of cooking. Cook the sugar syrup until it reaches 230°F (110°C), about 25 minutes, depending on your stove. Skim off any foam that rises to the top, and stir occasionally as the syrup cooks. Add the plums to the hot syrup and continue to cook until the mixture is 217°F (103°C), about 30 minutes longer. The mixture will thicken and the plums will become translucent. Turn the heat to low. No additional pectin is needed.

During the last few minutes of cooking, turn up the heat under the jars and add clean lids to the boiling water. Remove a jar and a lid from the water (special jar-lifting tongs are available, but you can use regular metal tongs). Using a ladle, pour the preserves through a widemouthed funnel into the jar. Fill the jar to within ¼ inch of the top. Wipe the top of the jar and the rubber seal on the lid with a towel. Screw on the lid. Fill the rest of the jars. Return the filled jars to the pot of water. They should not touch each other, nor should they touch the bottom or sides of the pot. Add enough additional water to cover the jars by 1 inch.

Bring the water to a boil, and boil the jars for 20 minutes. Add 5 minutes for each 2,000 feet of elevation above sea level.

After processing, let the jars cool on a towel. When they are completely cool, check the seal on each one. The center of the lid will be depressed if the lid has sealed properly. If a jar did not seal, refrigerate it and consume the contents within a week. Store the sealed jars in a cool, dark place. They will keep for at least a year, providing breakfast treats on a moment's notice.

Sugar Plum Cakes

The ancient practice of preserving fruit in alcohol allows you to make these cakes when the fruit is no longer in season. I thought of this idea one summer when I had a surplus of plums from my friend Jerome's tree.

Note that the plums need to soak about 3 months before use. The simple task of preserving plums in August allows you to make these cakes for the winter holiday season.

Preserve the plums

In the late summer, gather the ripest, most flavorful plums you can find. You will need 8 or 9 plums to make 2 cakes, but as these make wonderful gifts, preserve a few jars of fruit. Wash them and put them in clean quart jars. Fill the jars with vodka (inexpensive vodka is fine), and add ⅓ cup granulated sugar to each jar. Cover the jars tightly and store in a cool, dark place. After 3 days, if the sugar has not dissolved, turn the jars over a few times. Repeat every 3 days until the sugar dissolves, then leave them undisturbed until November or December, when you can use the plums to make the cakes.

2 CAKES, BAKED IN 3-CUP RING MOLDS

1 cup (5 ounces) unbleached all purpose flour
¼ cup (1¼ ounces) white cornmeal
¼ teaspoon salt
1 teaspoon baking powder
14 tablespoons (7 ounces) unsalted butter at room temperature
¾ cup (6 ounces) granulated sugar
2 extra-large eggs at room temperature
8 or 9 preserved plums, pitted and coarsely chopped (¾ cup or 7 ounces)
2 tablespoons liquid from the plums
Powdered sugar, for dusting

Preheat the oven to 350°F.

Generously butter two 3-cup ring molds.

Sift together the flour, cornmeal, salt, and baking powder, and set aside.

Beat the butter in the bowl of a heavy-duty mixer with the paddle attachment until it is soft. Add the sugar and beat until fluffy. Whisk the eggs in a small bowl. With the mixer running, add the eggs very slowly to the butter-sugar mixture, a fourth at a time, allowing the batter to incorporate each addition before continuing. Add the dry ingredients to the batter, then the plums and 2 tablespoons of their liquid.

Distribute the batter between the molds, set them on a baking tray and place it on the middle shelf of the oven.

Bake the cakes until they are browned and a skewer inserted into them comes out clean, 55 to 60 minutes. Cool to lukewarm, then turn them out of the molds. When they are completely cool, dust with powdered sugar. They will keep refrigerated and wrapped in plastic for 1 week. To give as gifts, envelop them in colored cellophane and tie them with ribbons.

EVE'S FRUIT

I HOPED THAT MY EYES WERE DECEIVING ME. It's a fifty-foot drop
from the deck of our country house to the small orchard below, and red-
wood trees obscure some of the view. But when I looked again, I knew
that the branch's sharp angle could mean only one thing—it had snapped
from the weight of the fruit. I felt like one of my own limbs was broken.
It was the first time that my three-year-old quince tree had fruited,
yielding nine fragrant gems. I walked down the curving path with my
basket and Felco pruner, gathered the quinces, and pruned the remaining
branches, probably cutting off next year's fruit buds but giving the tree a
healthier shape.

Had I lived in colonial America, I probably wouldn't have worried as
much about my quince tree. Either I would have had more than one or
my neighbors could have supplied me with fruit from their orchards. Like
most women of the time, I would have mastered sugar cooking and
quince preparation. Sugar wasn't the same then; it was not as refined and
still contained impurities. Before being combined with the fruit, it had to
be clarified—boiled with water, skimmed of the black scum that rose to
the surface, and mixed with egg whites, which latched onto other impurities so they could be discarded. With the sugar clarified, I would have
had many choices: slowly cooking quinces with sugar until the mass was
stiff enough to stand on its own, then letting it cool and cutting it into
cubes; or making crystal clear jelly from quince cooking liquid and sugar;
or making marmalade.

The marmalade would have required the most skill. Women of the
period prided themselves on their marmalade. I would have even had
musk, ambergris, and eryngo roots in my larder, ingredients necessary to
make a very fancy version. Then, if I had any quinces left after putting up

quarts and quarts of marmalade, I could have cooked them in a strong broth made from old quinces and peelings and stored them in a jar. If mold grew on the top, I would have simply removed it, brought the fruit and liquid to a boil, and put it in a clean container, keeping the quinces all year to make tarts whenever I wanted one. A few perfect specimens could have rested in a bowl in the kitchen, their delicate fragrance perfuming the house. If I needed inspiration for a recipe, I could have consulted *Martha Washington's Booke of Cookery*, with its twenty-two recipes for quinces.

But it was in a produce store in San Francisco in 1985, not Virginia in 1785, that I first considered cooking quinces. I stood looking at a display of them, remembering the cubes of fruit essence I had bought in a Paris pastry shop. They had tasted like a cross between an apple and a pear, with another earthy flavor all its own that came alive just before swallowing. I bought a box of the fruit and took it to the bakery. The quinces looked like misshapen pears, rock hard, covered with a waxy fuzz, and very fragrant. I cut a piece from one and tasted it—astringent and mouth-puckering, nothing like what I had tasted in France. I could have used Martha's book that day. Lacking it, I looked through cookbooks until I found a recipe pairing quinces with lots of sugar and autumnal spices. We cooked the quinces for a long time, until the astringency transformed into the taste I remembered and the color changed dramatically from a pale yellow to a deep shade of burnt orange with red overtones. A tart filled with this compote seemed like a good idea. We lined tart pans with dough, spooned in the fruit, covered the top with a dough lattice, and then baked it until the crust was brown and the filling bubbling. Quince tarts came to signal autumn at the bakery, even more than pumpkins and cranberries. It was exciting to introduce this ancient fruit to customers, to watch them taste a sample and then break into a smile and exclaim, "That's good!" The tarts developed a stalwart following that awaited their arrival each fall.

Making a once-noble fruit popular again has its drawbacks. Finding enough quinces to make what had become our signature tarts was challenging. Pineapple quince, the variety most commonly available from commercial distributors, was not as flavorful as the first ones I bought at the produce store, which were from a backyard in Sonoma. I started looking for quince trees anytime we went outside the city. My diligence paid off. During a visit with a friend who lives in the wilds of Trinity County five hours north of San Francisco, I spotted quince trees in her orchard. She promised me some of the fall crop. The next October, she hauled four heavy boxes into the bakery, wondering if they were good enough to use. They were the definitive quinces, so aromatic and flavorful that others paled by comparison. Even though we kept them in a back storeroom, customers could smell them as soon as they walked in the door. My friend became a regular supplier.

During trips to the Anderson Valley, I found other sources, both commercial and backyard. An old-fashioned farm stand at a curve on Highway 128 sold quinces in the fall. And our friends at a winery on top of a ridge offered boxes from their fertile tree that I accepted gladly.

Unfortunately, I didn't discover the best commercial source until after the bakery closed. They were sold by the Kaprielian Brothers in Reedley, California. The company was started by three brothers who immigrated from Armenia at the beginning of the century, and it is still run by their successors. The fruit that I bought was my favorite variety, Smyrna, packed two deep in a heavy cardboard box. All the fruit was perfect—unblemished, a uniform yellow, and highly perfumed. Each quince was wrapped in a square of white tissue paper. A blue circle in the center of the paper announced "Grandma Ruth's Quince Recipes." Around the circle were recipes for baked quince, quince compote, sautéed quince, and caramelized quince, each listing ingredients and simple, straightforward instructions. There were also a few helpful hints—quince in a closet or cupboard will keep the air fresh, and quince can be kept for months in a bowl on the kitchen counter. This folksy way of making the fruit enticing wasn't a gimmick. There really was a Grandma Ruth, and these really were her recipes.

John Kaprielian remembers eating quinces as a child. His grandmother and mother cooked them in the fall, making quince butter, canning them like peaches, and baking them for Thanksgiving dinner. He is very fond of his wife's quince cobbler, and told me, "Once you eat quinces, you'll never eat apples again."

Desserts made from quinces are my favorite way to use this fruit. But last year I decided to experiment with some of the crop from my tree by trying savory preparations from the Middle East and South Africa. It made me excited about quinces all over again. I discovered a trick to convince modern palates, jaded by the sugar in today's diet, to embrace quinces cooked in savory dishes—I cook them with a little sugar first. Now, just as Eve probably tempted Adam with a quince, not an apple, I'll tempt my guests with savory quinces. I'm sure they'll find them irresistible.

Master Recipe for Quince

The recipes that follow are based on this master recipe for cooking quinces. After peeling boxes of quinces at the bakery, I decided that this step can be eliminated. Leaving the skin intact makes the preparation easier and intensifies their flavor. Because the fruit is so hard, a sharp knife and a steady hand are needed to cut it into chunks.

When quinces are in season, buy at least 3 pounds and cook them in a sugar syrup in the oven. They will keep, in the cooking syrup, for at least 3 weeks in the refrigerator. They can be heated and served alone, used to make a fruit compote with poached pears, cooked apples, and stewed prunes, or used in the recipes that follow. With a cooked supply on hand, the other recipes require minimal preparation.

ENOUGH FOR THE RECIPES THAT FOLLOW

3 pounds quinces (8 small)
1⅓ cups (9½ ounces) granulated sugar
1½ cups (12 ounces) water

Preheat the oven to 325°F.

Wash the quinces well to remove any dirt and fuzz. Leave the skins on but remove the cores. Because the fruit is very hard, a standard apple corer doesn't stand up to the job. It's easier to cut them into halves top to bottom and use a sturdy melon-baller to scrape out the cores. As you work, drop the cored quinces into water acidified with the juice of a lemon so they won't turn brown.

Bring the sugar and water to a boil in a medium-size flameproof casserole with a lid. Add the fruit and return the syrup to a boil again. Cover the casserole and put it in the middle of the oven. Bake the quinces until they turn a rosy hue but still hold their shape, 1½ to 2 hours.

Cool the quinces, then refrigerate them in the syrup until needed.

Cooked Quince
and Sweet Potato Gratin

Sweet potatoes aren't potatoes at all, and to further complicate matters, the darker, moist-fleshed sweet potatoes often called yams really aren't yams. Both the mealy sweet potatoes and the so-called yams are *Ipomoea batatas*, a member of the morning glory family. True yams belong to the family Dioscoreaceae.

The Garnet variety is a good choice for this gratin because it has an orange flesh that deepens in color as it cooks, complementing the color of the quinces. The slight sweetness of the quinces infuses the sweet potatoes during baking, deepening their flavor. (Maybe sweetening the sweet potatoes inspired the marshmallow-topped casserole of the 1950s that was served at my family Thanksgivings. I prefer this version.)

Sausages or smoked meats are a good match for this dish.

4 SERVINGS
> 1 tablespoon vegetable oil
> 1¼ pounds (1 large) Garnet sweet potato, peeled and sliced diagonally ¼ inch thick
> 3 cooked quince halves (see the master recipe), sliced ¼ inch thick
> Chicken or vegetable stock
> Salt and pepper

Preheat the oven to 375°F.

Oil the bottom of a medium-size flameproof gratin dish.

Put a row of sweet potatoes at the end of the gratin dish, overlapping them slightly at a 45° angle. Put a row of quince slices against the sweet potatoes. Continue alternating rows until the dish is full. Add enough stock to barely cover the contents. Season with salt and pepper. Bring the stock to a boil on the top of the stove.

Bake the gratin in the middle of the oven for 15 minutes. Remove it from the oven and push the vegetables down into the liquid with a spatula. Return it to the oven and continue baking until the potatoes are browned and soft when pierced with a skewer and the quinces are lightly caramelized, another 10 to 15 minutes. Serve the gratin hot.

BUCKWHEAT CREPES WITH QUINCE FILLING

Large, thin crêpes made of buckwheat flour are folded over savory fillings throughout Brittany, in the northwest corner of France. Instead of a savory filling, chopped cooked quinces fill these buckwheat cylinders. Serve them for breakfast or brunch.

A well-seasoned crêpe pan, 8½ inches in diameter, is the utensil of choice. Lacking one, use a well-seasoned skillet or a nonstick pan of about the same size.

To cook crêpes quickly, follow this method suggested by Marion Norberg, who tested this recipe: Use two pans, one the seasoned crêpe pan, the other an oiled skillet the same size or larger. Pour the batter into the seasoned pan. When it's ready to be turned, flip it over into the second pan, and start another crêpe while the first finishes cooking.

This recipe makes an ample amount of batter, in case some of the crêpes are less than perfect.

8 CRÊPES, 4 SERVINGS

> ¾ cup (4 ounces) unbleached all-purpose flour
> ¾ cup (4 ounces) buckwheat flour
> 1 teaspoon salt
> 1 extra-large egg
> About 1½ cups water
> 12 ounces (about 5 halves) cooked quinces (see the master recipe), chopped and warmed
> Cooking syrup from the quinces, heated
> Powdered sugar, for garnish

Make the crêpes

Combine the flours and salt in a medium-size bowl. In another bowl, beat the egg and 1 cup of the water with a fork. Pour this into the bowl with the flours and beat everything together, using the fork. Add additional water until the batter is the consistency of heavy cream.

Warm 4 serving plates plus 1 extra in an oven set at the lowest temperature.

Moisten a folded paper towel with vegetable oil and swab the inside of the pan. Heat it until a drop of water sizzles on its surface. Ladle about ¼ cup (2 ounces) of batter into the middle of the pan, then immediately tilt and rotate the pan to distribute the batter in a thin layer. Pour any excess back into the bowl. Cook the crêpe until the edges curl and the bottom browns and slides free of the pan, about 1 minute. Turn the crêpe over and cook the other side. Slide onto a waiting heated plate. Often the first crêpe isn't ideal. If it doesn't measure up, discard it.

Continue cooking crêpes, swabbing the pan each time with oil. Keep the cooked crêpes in the warm oven until you've made 8.

Fill the crêpes

The side of the crêpe that cooks second is not as attractive, so make that the inside. Put a spoonful of quince at the edge of each crêpe and roll it into a cylinder. Put two rolled crêpes in the middle of each serving plate, seam side down. Spoon warmed cooking syrup around them. Sift powdered sugar over the crêpes and serve immediately.

QUINCE AND APPLE PINWHEEL GALETTES

Quince and apple slices alternate atop a piece of sweet dough, catching the eye with their contrasting colors and piquing the taste buds with their sweet and earthy flavors. The dough is easy to make and can be used for other sweet tarts. There will be some left over.

I like Sierra Beauty or Pink Pearl apples for this recipe. Use locally grown apples if possible.

6 SERVINGS

The galette dough

12 tablespoons (6 ounces) unsalted butter at room temperature
½ cup (3½ ounces) granulated sugar
1 extra-large egg
½ teaspoon vanilla extract
1¾ cups (8½ ounces) unbleached all-purpose flour

The fruit

3 locally grown apples
6 cooked quince halves (see the master recipe)
Cooking syrup from the quinces
½ cup (4 ounces) heavy whipping cream
1 teaspoon powdered sugar

Make the galette dough

Place the butter in the bowl of a heavy-duty mixer. Beat with the paddle until it is creamy. Add the sugar and beat until light and fluffy. In a separate bowl, beat the egg and vanilla together with a fork. With the mixer running, add the egg. Scrape the bowl and mix well. Add the flour all at once, and mix until the ingredients are just incorporated. Remove the dough from the bowl, flatten it to a thickness of ½ inch on a piece of plastic wrap, cover it with more plastic wrap, and refrigerate for 1 hour, or up to 3 days. The dough can also be frozen, tightly wrapped, for 1 month.

Assemble and bake the galettes

Preheat the oven to 375°F.

Roll the chilled dough to a ⅛-inch thickness on a lightly floured surface. Cut into disks, 5½ inches in diameter, and lay them on a parchment-lined baking sheet. Refrigerate until the fruit is ready.

Peel the apples. Cut them in half, from top to bottom, through the cores. Remove the cores. (A melon baller does this job best.) Place them cut side down on a work surface and slice thinly.

Peel the quince halves (the skin should slip off easily). Place them cut side down on a work surface and slice them thinly.

Remove the baking sheet holding the dough rounds from the refrigerator. Arrange the fruit in a pinwheel in the center of each piece of dough, alternating quince and apple slices. Carefully brush the fruit with the quince cooking syrup.

Bake the *galettes* until the pastry is browned and the apples are soft, 20 to 25 minutes. Remove them from the oven and let cool. Brush them again with the quince cooking syrup.

Whip the cream with the sugar until soft peaks form.

Serve the cooled *galettes* with a dollop of whipped cream on the side of the plate.

PUREE OF COOKED QUINCES AND CELERY ROOT

This was inspired by a recipe in Michel Guérard's book *La Cuisine Gourmande*.

The cooked quinces add a blush of color and a delicate, underlying taste to the forthright celery root. Don't be alarmed if the milk curdles during cooking. It will become smooth again in the food processor.

For a new taste, substitute this for mashed potatoes in your favorite menu.

4 SERVINGS

10 ounces (half of a medium-size) celery root, peeled and sliced
5 ounces (1 small cooked) quince (see the master recipe), sliced
About 2 cups (16 ounces) whole milk
Salt and white pepper

Place the celery root and the cooked quince in a medium-size saucepan. Add the milk and simmer until the celery root is soft, about 20 minutes.

Transfer the celery root and quince to a food processor. With the motor running, add enough of the milk to make a smooth purée. Add salt and pepper to taste. Serve hot.

OLIVE OIL ARTISANS

I WAS A LATE CONVERT TO OLIVE OIL. We ate margarine during my childhood, not as a healthy choice (saturated fat and cholesterol were only words in the dictionary then), but because it was less expensive. I remember squeezing those little capsules of orange liquid onto bricks of white fat and massaging in the color so it looked like real butter. But it really didn't. The vibrant color gave it away. The only time I remember eating butter when I was growing up was with holiday meals. Years later, when I became interested in French cooking, I turned to butter. This was when every recipe started with, "Melt 1 stick of butter in a saucepan." Margarine wasn't mentioned. Neither was olive oil.

But olive oil crept slowly into our lives. For years, we used it mostly for vinaigrette. Gradually, we began putting it to other uses as well—as a sauté medium and brushed onto vegetables before grilling. At the bakery, we bought cases of prudently priced Spanish oil that got mixed into our *fougasse* dough.

These days, olive oil connoisseurs have many choices: oils imported from various countries, both expensive extra-virgin and those priced for everyday use, and a rebirth of California oil. Not that cooking is the best use for some of this oil. The high prices commanded by McEvoy and DaVero oils, cold-pressed from trees imported from Tuscany, put them in a different category from cooking oil of any type. This is "condiment oil," used sparingly to accent salad greens or to anoint grilled fish (after it's grilled, not before). The 1997 DaVero Dry Creek Valley olive oil, sounding more like a wine than an oil, was the first American olive oil to be given extra-virgin status by the International Olive Oil Council. It is also the first American extra-virgin olive oil to win a blind tasting in Italy. It took years of nurturing the orchards before they produced any oil at all, let alone win a prestigious award.

Nan McEvoy hand-picked her first trees in Italy with the help of an Italian expert. Now she has almost eleven thousand, many propagated on her ranch, covering rolling hills in west Marin County, north of San Francisco. When she bought the land, it wasn't to plant orchards, but she had to demonstrate an agricultural use to refurbish some of the buildings and, not wanting cows (the site had been a dairy ranch), she turned to olives. Now, the Marin Agricultural Land Trust, an organization devoted to preserving agricultural land by acquiring conservation easements, gives tours of the McEvoy ranch. Sidney and I joined a group one Saturday morning. The woman leading the tour let it be known from the outset that they don't even consider some popular Italian brands found in supermarkets to be olive oil.

The first trees were planted in 1992. Although they arrived with identification tags, many tags were lost during the mandatory agricultural inspection, so those first rows are a mix. Subsequent rows are planted with a single variety, including Leccino, Frantoio, and Pendolino. Even though olive trees are drought resistant, these trees are irrigated to ensure good yields—but knowing the correct amount of water is tricky. Too much and the olives won't be as good. It took four years to get a sizable crop. During the first harvest, workers laid tarpaulins under the trees and picked the fruit by hand. Now they use pneumatic combs from Italy, a more efficient method. After harvest the olives are processed in the milling and extraction room, situated in a large building next to the orchard. There is nothing makeshift here. State-of-the-art equipment from Italy stands ready, even though it is used only one month of the year. I didn't want to think about the price of these machines. After washing, the whole olives are crushed, pits and all, either under huge granite stones, or in a hammer mill. Then a machine called a maxillator kneads the resulting paste. The next step, spreading the paste on mats, stacking them in a press, and applying pressure to extract oil and water from the solids, has been practiced in every olive-producing country for millennia. I looked around for the mats, but there weren't any. Instead, the paste goes into a more modern machine, where stainless steel blades work through it. Only oil clings to the blades; about 20 percent of the oil is extracted this way. Another machine separates the rest of the liquid from the solids, then vertical centrifuges separate the oil from the water. This cold-pressed oil never exceeds 86°F (30°C). Its acidity level, 0.2 percent, is well below the 1 percent standard for extra-virgin oil. With a yield of thirty gallons of oil from one ton of fruit, this is an expensive endeavor.

Oils in California didn't always have an Italian pedigree. Franciscan fathers, led by Junípero Serra, established Mission San Diego de Alcalá in California in 1769. Within twenty years, olives were being grown there, and by 1803 very good oil was reportedly being made. The practice of growing olives, both from cuttings and seedlings, spread to the other missions in California. But olive oil production had its problems. When the missions passed into secular hands, care of the orchards declined. Many were revived, but the price of the oil was undercut by imported oil. Eventually, the bulk of the olives wound up in cans, with four cultivars dominating—Mission, Manzanillo, Sevillano, and Ascolano.

People are still producing oil from these cultivars. The Sciabica family in Modesto has been in business for sixty years, making extra-virgin oil from the older Spanish olives, identifying them by harvest, and keeping some unfiltered.

Steve Tylicki, a vineyard consultant in the Anderson Valley, is encouraging the planting of olive trees. For him, the transition from vines to olives was logical; both are farmed in a similar fashion, and the sensory evaluation is the same. Sidney and I went to his oil tasting at the Anderson Valley Pinot Noir Weekend. Each participant got three oils in glasses tinted dark blue so the color wouldn't influence the taste. We cupped our hands over the tops and swirled the oil to bring it to room temperature. Next we took some in our mouths and aerated it as if it were wine. Then we swallowed. Steve stressed that unlike wine tasting, the oil must be swallowed to really get the full taste. People made gurgling noises and coughed. After two of the selections, I was beginning to feel well oiled. Steve gave us sheets with descriptives for the oils to help us identify characteristics—aroma (apple, other fruit, bitter, pungent, sweet);

taste (sour, rough, metallic, peppery, musty, and fusty, used to describe olives that sat around too long before being pressed). He is on his way to becoming a certified olive oil taster, and then he can sit on panels to judge oils applying for certification.

Where is all this oil going? More people are cooking with olive oil. Over the last decade, health concerns have converted many people from butter to olive oil, with its unsaturated fatty acids. The monounsaturates in the oil may even reduce harmful cholesterol, the national obsession. In many San Francisco restaurants, the emphasis on Mediterranean cooking probably accounts for gallons of olive oil a day.

Lou Preston, the owner of Preston Vineyards in the Dry Creek Valley, leaves the winemaking to his wine maker these days. Lou spends his time baking bread in his new wood-fired oven, experimenting with olive curing, and thinking about the blend for the next olive oil bottling. He isn't nationalistic about the choice of olives. Some come from the Mission and Manzanillo trees, originally intended for decoration, that he planted fifteen years ago. Others are from Italian varieties that he suitcased into the country. He propagated all of the trees over the years and in 1992 had enough olives to press into oil. Rather than invest in pressing equipment, he sends the fruit to Frantoio restaurant, where it is pressed for him. He calls the oil Olio Luigi, il Promìscuo, reflecting the eyebrow-raising practice of blending the old California olives with the Italian ones. The 1997 vintage has recently received extra-virgin certification from the Certification Board of the California Olive Oil Council, which uses the same criteria as in Italy. He shared his tasting notes with me—"light, green-gold color. Fresh, fruity, ripe olive/green apple aroma with delicate floral notes, medium bodied with a slightly peppery finish. Sounds Tuscan, doesn't it?" That virtue will probably help its selling price.

Although I use olive oil more and more, I always have three or four pounds of unsalted butter in my freezer. All pastry demands it, and many dishes need just a touch of its special unctuousness. When my butter consumption starts to exceed healthy limits, I think more of olive oil. And it's an easy decision to forego an eight-ounce steak for a piece of good pastry.

BRUSCHETTA WITH ANCHOVIES

Showcase your best extra-virgin olive oil (the country of origin is up to you) with these beguilingly delicious but easy-to-make appetizers. The ingredients must be of the highest quality for these to shine. As much as I love sourdough bread, its tang competes with the olive oil, so a rustic loaf that isn't sour is a better choice. The garlic is important too. Use fresh-tasting garlic that isn't bitter. I recently bought garlic at a farmers' market from a woman who has been growing the same variety for twenty years. The only problem is that she can't remember the name. It was still fresh and had a clean, haunting sweetness. The hardneck French Rocambole, with its coiled flower stalks and deep flavor, is another of my favorites. Plump anchovies packed in olive oil and imported from Italy are the ones to use.

4 APPETIZER SERVINGS
> 8 slices (½ inch thick) rustic country bread
> 1 large clove garlic, cut in half
> About ¼ cup (2 ounces) extra-virgin olive oil
> 8 or more anchovy fillets, drained on a paper towel

If you have a hot charcoal fire, grill both sides of the bread over it. If not, use a toaster. While the bread is still warm, vigorously rub the cut garlic half over one side of each slice. Drizzle the same side with olive oil. Top each with an anchovy or two, draped lengthwise on the bread. Serve immediately.

FOUGASSE

Fougasse is a fanciful flatbread originating in the south of France. It is slashed before baking so it resembles a ladder or a tree. Although different doughs can be used, this one contains olive oil, garlic, and rosemary, typical flavorings in Provence.

TWO FLATBREADS

> 6 tablespoons (3 ounces) olive oil
> 1 clove garlic, finely chopped
> 2 tablespoons chopped fresh rosemary
> 1⅔ cups (13 ounces) cold tap water
> 2½ teaspoons active dry yeast
> 4½ cups (1 pound 7 ounces) unbleached all-purpose flour
> 2 teaspoons salt
> 1 tablespoon coarse sea salt

Make the dough

Simmer the olive oil, garlic, and rosemary in a small pan for 30 seconds. Set aside and let cool to room temperature.

Pour the water into the bowl of a heavy-duty mixer. Sprinkle the yeast over the water and wait until it dissolves and becomes creamy, about 5 minutes. Add the cooled flavored oil mixture, then the flour and the 2 teaspoons salt. Knead the dough at medium speed for 8 minutes, adding more flour or water if needed. The dough will form a ball, but will be soft and a little sticky. Cover the bowl with plastic wrap and leave it at room temperature (75°F) until the dough doubles, 2½ to 3 hours.

Shape the dough

Turn the dough onto a floured work surface. Divide it into halves. Shape each piece into a ball. Cover the balls with plastic wrap or a kitchen towel and let them rest for 5 minutes. Flatten each piece into an elongated round with your hands. Make cuts in the dough with a pizza cutter. For a tree shape, make a 2-inch cut in the center about 1 inch below the top. Then make 2 diagonal cuts on each side slanting toward the center. To shape a ladder, make 4 diagonal cuts down the center of the dough. Pick up each piece and rap it on the work surface a few times to separate the cuts. Put the shapes on a parchment-lined baking sheet, then slide the baking sheet into a plastic bag and leave at room temperature until the dough doubles, about 1½ hours.

Bake the fougasses

Place a large, empty baking pan at the lowest level of the oven. Preheat the oven to 425°F.

When the loaves are ready for the oven, bring 2 cups water to a boil.

Remove the baking sheet from the plastic bag. Mist the loaves with water and sprinkle with the coarse sea salt. Put the sheet on the middle shelf of the oven. Immediately pour the boiling water into the empty pan in the bottom of the oven and close the door. *Caution:* This will cause an immediate burst of steam. Wear long oven mitts and stand back to avoid being burned. Don't open the door for the first 10 minutes or the steam will escape.

Bake the fougasses until they are nicely browned and sound hollow when thumped on the bottom, 30 minutes. Cool them on a rack.

Fougasses can be served cut, split, or whole to be torn with the fingers.

RED PEPPER AND OLIVE OIL SAUCE

Use meaty red bell, gypsy, or pimiento peppers and your best olive oil to make this versatile sauce. Then toss it with pasta, spoon it on roasted potatoes, or serve it as an accompaniment to grilled vegetables, chicken, or fish.

ABOUT 1⅔ CUPS

4 red peppers (about 1½ pounds)
1 teaspoon Dijon-style mustard
2 teaspoons balsamic vinegar
½ cup (4 ounces) extra-virgin olive oil
Dash ground cayenne pepper, or to taste

Heat the peppers over a gas stove burner (or under a broiler) until they are completely charred. Put them in a paper bag. When they are cool, remove the skins under running water. Discard the stems, inside ribs, and seeds.

Place the peppers in a food processor fitted with a steel blade. Add the mustard. With the processor running, add the vinegar, then slowly drizzle the olive oil through the feed tube. Process until smooth. Add the cayenne. Transfer the sauce to a serving dish.

Vegetarian Turkey

THANKSGIVING DINNER IS ALWAYS AT OUR HOUSE. We have cooked turkeys every way possible—in an O'Keefe and Merritt oven, starting breast side down, basting frequently; in our commercial convection oven, which produced the crispiest skin; in a Weber barbecue; in *nouvelle cuisine* fashion, cutting up the bird, roasting the breast meat, and eating that as one course while the legs continued to cook; after a twenty-four-hour brine treatment; and in our outdoor adobe oven at our country house. Friends bring other components of the meal, but Sidney and I are always in charge of the bird.

Usually ten to fifteen people sit down at the table. During the years when the children were young, it was a boisterous affair, parents cutting up food and mediating disagreements, and usually at least one parent missing, soothing a fretful infant. As the children grew, it was the adults who talked and laughed the loudest, fueled by special bottles of wine that everyone brought from their cellars. During their high school years, the kids ate politely, and then escaped as soon as possible, to congregate in Casey and Claire's rooms, playing guitars, listening to music, or watching television.

Then last year, Sidney and I faced a special Thanksgiving dilemma—all the teenagers had become vegetarians. Turkey was out. Tofu was in. The change was predictable with Claire, our animal-loving daughter. First she stopped eating red meat. But chickens were still acceptable; she would still carve the ones we frequently roasted for dinner, vying with her brother for the "oysters," the sweet morsels on either side of the backbone. "It's because they're so stupid," she explained. "Cows are smart?" I asked myself. But over time chickens were excluded too. Claire would still eat cheese, eggs, and selected vegetables, and she had never liked fish of any kind.

Casey's conversion took a different course. It was a radical, blink-of-the-eye change. Before he left for college, he was a junk food maven, although he also appreciated well-prepared food, especially large steaks. Then he moved to Santa Cruz, one of the last bastions of hippiedom in the state, to attend the university there. In a flash, he was buying bagfuls of vegetables and shopping at the organic farmers' market. All meat was out. He actually cooked and ate tofu. I love vegetables and probably eat more than the rest of my family combined, but I draw the line at tofu.

Our friends' daughters were on the same food trajectory. And to bolster the vegetarian ranks, Casey had invited a friend from school for dinner. For me, the meal had to be as special as it had always been; relegating them to eating side dishes of vegetables wouldn't be a Thanksgiving dinner. We had to come up with something spectacular that would please everyone. The thinking process began. We had a month.

I leafed through the vegetable sections of cookbooks without inspiration. The vegetarians couldn't help. When asked for ideas, they were mute. "Just cook a bunch of vegetables, Mom," was their answer. A bunch of vegetables for Thanksgiving dinner? We could do better—but what?

Two weeks went by. We were at a standstill. Various vegetable casseroles and exotic lasagnes didn't seem right. Then one evening, Sidney, returning from a business trip, burst into the house. "I have it, I have it!" he yelled as he ran up the stairs. "What are you talking about?" I asked. "Thanksgiving dinner. Let's make a *timpano*! Remember the *timpano* that Primo made in the movie *Big Night*? It came to me on the plane, sandwiched in the middle seat between two large people. It would be perfect." I thought about the film and recalled the triumphant moment when the *timpano* was brought to the table, a browned dome enveloping layers of goodness. It almost looked like a turkey. This could be the answer.

We struggled to remember the preparation from the movie, but the details eluded us. I looked through all our Italian cookbooks. There was only one vague reference to a *timpano*. Then we took a life-imitates-art approach and rented the movie, replaying the frames that included the dish. One scene showed a sheet of pasta lining a bowl and being filled with sautéed mushrooms, cooked pasta, other vegetables; another shot showed an unmolded *timpano* with compressed individual pieces of pasta making up the outside layer. We would have to experiment, preferably before our big night.

The enclosing outside layer generated the most discussion. Individual pieces of pasta seemed too risky; the whole thing might come tumbling down. A sheet of pasta was one idea; thinly rolled puff pastry another. We decided to make one of each, and knowing that there would be ample food, invited another couple for dinner to help us finalize the recipe.

The Ferry Plaza Farmers' Market provided ingredients: a sheet of egg pasta, red pepper rigatoni and garlic pasta spirals, shiitake and chanterelle mushrooms, kale and chard, leeks, carrots, oregano, sage, and parsley. I had chestnuts from the Twenty-Second and Irving Market that I roasted and peeled, and puff pastry from the Downtown Bakery. We chopped and sautéed the vegetables, cooked the individual pastas, and hard-boiled some eggs. Sidney, the resident saucier, made béchamel and tomato sauces.

Timpano #1 was the pasta version. First we brushed a stainless bowl with olive oil and draped the sheet of pasta inside. Then we layered in the ingredients, all four of us in the action. This one held kale, shiitakes, rigatoni moistened with tomato sauce, leeks, and sliced cooked eggs, with freshly chopped parsley and oregano as seasonings. When the bowl was full, we folded the excess pasta over the filling and drizzled on more olive oil. A piece of foil covered the pasta.

Timpano #2 had a puff pastry lining. Butter replaced the olive oil to brush the bowl. The filling was different—chard, chanterelles, chestnuts, the spiral pastas in bèchamel, carrots, a few leeks, parsley, and sage. As with the first *timpano*, the pastry covered the filling and foil covered the pastry.

While our creations baked, we made a green salad and opened another bottle of wine. Since all the ingredients except the outside layers were already cooked, we decided that a piping-hot internal temperature of 160 degrees would be sufficient. Sidney took the hot bowls from the oven and removed the foil. Then with a quick flick of the wrist he overturned each one onto a platter. We all held our breath. Were the linings fused to the bowls? What luck—they came off easily. Both *timpanos* were a rich brown. If I squinted, they almost looked like roasted turkey breasts.

A lively discussion of the merits of each took place over the dinner table, as we tasted back and forth. The pasta lining of *timpano #1* was a little brittle; everyone preferred the puff pastry. The filling of the puff pastry version seemed more balanced, the sweetness of the chestnuts and carrots and the earthiness of the chanterelles a good counterpoint to the creamy pasta. We declared *timpano #2* the winner.

When I told Casey and Claire that we had found something special for Thanksgiving dinner, they were skeptical. Efforts to keep them out of the kitchen during *timpano* preparations were futile. They peeked at every chance and withheld judgment. But when the bowl was lifted from the steaming pièce de résistance, it caught their attention. Sidney had toyed with the idea of adding balls of fried tofu to the platter to simulate drumsticks, but we didn't have any in the house. The vegetarians' fears faded when they tasted the *timpano*. They all ate seconds, as well as large helpings of watercress and apple salad and pumpkin bread, but left room for small slivers of apple pie and quince tart.

I loved the *timpano*. It will be the centerpiece of future Thanksgiving dinners, as long as vegetarians join us at the table. But I also liked the small turkey that we smoked in our new barbecue.

Watercress Salad with Apples, Pecans, and a Pecan Oil Vinaigrette

Use locally grown apples for this fall salad as part of a Thanksgiving dinner. Double the recipe if you have a crowd.

The California Press, in Rutherford, California, sells wonderful pecan oil in opaque ceramic bottles that keep out the light. If you can't find high-quality pecan oil, use a good olive oil instead.

5 SERVINGS

3 bunches watercress, washed and dried
1 large apple, cored and cut into ½-inch dice
⅓ cup (1½ ounces) coarsely chopped pecans, lightly toasted
⅛ teaspoon Dijon-style mustard
1 tablespoon red wine vinegar, 7% acidity
2 tablespoons pecan oil
2 tablespoons flavorless vegetable oil, such as canola
Salt and pepper

Place the watercress, apple, and pecans in a salad bowl. In a separate bowl, whisk the mustard and vinegar together, then whisk in the oils. Add salt and pepper to taste. Dress the salad and serve.

Vegetable Timpano

Both vegetarians and omnivores loved this dish when we made it the showpiece of a Thanksgiving dinner.

The basic notion is to cook a variety of vegetables separately, as well as a pound of pasta with a sauce to match. Everything is layered in a stainless steel bowl lined with puff pastry. The *timpano* is baked until the pastry is browned and the filling is hot, and then turned out as a radiant golden dome. I like the combination of ingredients in this one, but, using these general proportions, you could come up with other matches that are equally tasty. The vegetables can be cooked a day ahead.

If you use shelled chestnuts, buy the vacuum-packed nuts from France, available in specialty food stores. They are superior to canned chestnuts.

Buy the puff pastry from your favorite bakery.

10 TO 12 SERVINGS

The vegetables
> 1 large bunch (1¼ pounds) Swiss chard
> 1¼ pounds chanterelle mushrooms (or shiitake or oyster)
> Salt and pepper
> 6 large carrots (1 pound)
> 1 large onion (½ pound)
> 4 cloves garlic
> 2 tablespoons olive oil
> 1 pound in-the-shell chestnuts, or ½ pound shelled chestnuts
> ¼ cup finely chopped parsley
> 1 tablespoon finely chopped fresh sage

The pasta and béchamel sauce
> 1 pound dried pasta with an interesting shape
> 2 cups (16 ounces) whole milk
> 3 tablespoons (1½ ounces) butter

3 tablespoons all-purpose flour
Salt and pepper
Freshly grated nutmeg

The enveloping crust

2 pounds puff pastry made with butter

Cook the vegetables

Wash and roughly chop the Swiss chard. Put it in a large skillet and add enough water to cover the chard halfway. Season with salt and pepper. Cover and cook until the chard is soft, about 8 minutes. Drain and reserve.

Wipe the mushrooms with a damp cloth. Tear them into medium-size pieces. Heat a large nonstick skillet over high heat. Add half of the mushrooms and cook, shaking the pan frequently, until they give off their liquid and reduce by half in size. Transfer that batch to a bowl and cook the rest of the mushrooms. When they are all cooked, add salt and pepper to taste.

Peel the carrots. Cut each in half lengthwise, then thinly slice them. Boil the slices in salted water until they are tender. Drain and reserve.

Roughly chop the onion and garlic. Heat the olive oil in a large skillet. Add the onion and garlic, and sauté until soft but not browned. Salt and pepper to taste. Set aside.

If using chestnuts in the shell, make a cross with a sharp knife in the flat side of each one. Roast them in a 400°F oven until the cut shells pull away from the nuts. Remove from the oven and cover with a kitchen towel to keep them hot. As soon as you can handle them, peel away the outer shell and the papery skin underneath. Work with a few at a time, keeping the rest in the roasting pan. If they cool completely, they will be impossible to shell. If this happens, put them back in the oven for a few minutes, then try again.

Roughly chop the peeled nuts (either fresh or purchased).

Cook the pasta and make the béchamel sauce

Cook the pasta in a large quantity of salted boiling water until it is just al dente. Drain and rinse the pieces to keep them from sticking together. Set the pasta aside.

Heat the milk until it is hot but not simmering. Melt the butter in a heavy-bottomed saucepan. Add the flour to the butter and cook, whisking, until the flour is cooked but not browned, about 1 minute. Add the milk all at once and cook until it boils, whisking constantly. Add salt, pepper, and a little freshly grated nutmeg. Cover the sauce and set it aside.

Assemble and bake the *timpano*

Preheat the oven to 400°F.

Generously butter a 4-quart stainless steel bowl. If the puff pastry is in one piece, cut it into halves. Roll both pieces on a floured surface to a thickness of ⅛ inch. Go back and forth between the two pieces, allowing them to rest. Put one into the bowl, one edge overlapping the center by 1 inch, the other edge draping over the edge of the bowl. Put the second piece in the bowl, overlapping the first by 2 inches.

Mix the béchamel sauce and pasta together. If the sauce has become too thick, heat it gently to thin it. It must not be hot.

Alternately layer the cooked, cooled vegetables, mushrooms, chestnuts, parsley and sage, and pasta in the pastry-lined bowl, making two layers of each ingredient and ending with a layer of pasta.

Fold the pastry draping over the bowl into the center to overlap the vegetables. Cover the bowl with foil.

Bake the *timpano* until the internal temperature is 160°F, 1½ to 2 hours. During the last 20 minutes, remove the foil and increase the oven temperature to 425°F to brown the pastry.

Remove the bowl from the oven and let it cool for 20 minutes. Place a serving platter upside down on top of the bowl. Using an oven mitt, grasp the bowl and turn it over onto the platter. This may take two people. Remove the bowl and "carve" the *timpano* at the table.

PUMPKIN BREAD

This recipe was inspired by an old French recipe for a yeast-risen pumpkin bread made during the seventeenth century at Versailles. I've never seen a bread like this in France today, but it certainly goes well with an American Thanksgiving turkey, either in a stuffing or just as it is. Because the dough is shaped to look like pumpkins, one of the loaves would make a fanciful table decoration. It also makes great cheese sandwiches or *toast aux champignons*—mushrooms, herbed and quickly sautéed served over a slice of toasted bread.

2 LOAVES

> 2½ teaspoons active dry yeast
> ⅔ cup (5 ounces) cold tap water
> 2 cups (1 pound) canned cooked pumpkin, one small can
> 1 teaspoon grated nutmeg
> ½ teaspoon ground black pepper
> 1 tablespoon salt
> 5 cups (1 pound 9 ounces) unbleached all-purpose flour

Make the dough

Sprinkle the yeast over the water in the bowl of a heavy-duty mixer and wait until it dissolves and becomes creamy, about 5 minutes. Add the pumpkin and mix it in with a spatula. Toss the nutmeg, pepper, and salt with the flour and add to the bowl. Using a dough hook, mix everything together, then knead on medium speed for 10 minutes, adding flour if the dough sticks to the sides of the bowl. The dough should form a ball on the hook, but may not completely come away from the bottom of the bowl.

Cover the bowl with plastic wrap, and let the dough rise at room temperature until doubled, about 3 hours.

Shape the dough

Turn the dough onto a lightly floured surface and divide it into 2 pieces, reserving a small amount for the decorative tops. Form each piece into a round and place on a parchment-lined baking sheet. Roll the reserved dough into a cylinder 1 inch in diameter. Cut it into 2 pieces, each about 2 inches long. Make an indentation in the top of each round and push a piece of the cylinder, cut side up, into the round to attach the "stem" of the pumpkin. Stand a few tall glasses on the baking sheet, then slide it into a large plastic bag. (The glasses will keep the dough from sticking to the plastic.) Let the rounds rise at room temperature until almost doubled in bulk, 1½ to 2 hours.

Bake the bread

Place a large, empty baking pan at the lowest level of the oven. Preheat the oven to 425°F.

When the loaves are ready, bring 2 cups water to a boil.

Carefully remove the baking sheet from the plastic bag. Remove the glasses. With a sharp knife or a razor blade cut 5 vertical lines in each loaf from "stem" to bottom. Place the baking sheet in the oven. Immediately pour the hot water into the pan in the bottom of the oven, and close the door. *Caution:* This will cause an immediate burst of steam. Wear long oven mitts and stand back to avoid being burned. Don't open the door until the steam dissipates, about 10 minutes.

Bake the loaves until they are browned and sound hollow when tapped on the bottom, about 35 minutes. Cool before slicing.

APPLE FARMERS

IT WAS A SUNDAY AFTERNOON IN AUGUST, and we were beginning the drive back to the city after a weekend at our house in the Anderson Valley. Sidney turned left into the Apple Farm's driveway and stopped at the outdoor stand. There was just enough room in the trunk for two cases of apples, squeezed in front of the cooler, the luggage, and our teenagers' guitars, backpacks, tapes, and CDs.

Next to the bin of Gravensteins was an apple new to me, called Pink Pearl. It wasn't as pretty as the Gravensteins, with their red striping. The new apple was a uniform cream color, with a faint pink blush barely visible under the skin. Karen Bates, who runs the farm with her husband, Tim, emerged from the shed. I asked her about the Pink Pearls. She cut one open for me to taste. Exposing its flesh completely changed the apple's personality—it was a vibrant pink, the color of cotton candy. And it had a gutsy taste to match—crisp, firm, and tart. I bought some, along with a box of Gravensteins. At the bakery, we fanned slices of Pink Pearls on tarts and made others into apple rounds, disks of thin *croissant* dough with a pinwheel of apples baked on top. Their striking color wasn't diminished by cooking. I added Pink Pearls to my list of apple favorites.

Visits to the Apple Farm make me remember that apples are a fruit with a season, just like peaches, plums, and nectarines. From March to the end of July, juice, cider, and chutneys are available at their fruit stand. But there aren't any fresh apples. Meanwhile, apple bins in Bay Area supermarkets are full year-round. The shoppers expect them; apple pies aren't considered seasonal anymore. The supermarket varieties are limited to those that store or ship well. When the Washington supply wanes, the New Zealand apples arrive. Unfortunately, the unique ones, the best-tasting ones, have disappeared from the commercial market. Gone are the days when almost every homesteader had at least one apple tree, and gone are the markets of the early 1900s when nearly a thousand varieties were available.

Karen and Tim moved to the Apple Farm with their two small children in 1984 and, although they initially knew nothing about farming, slowly turned the disheveled property around. They brought neglected trees back to life, grafted older trees over to new varieties, and planted new blocks from scratch. Now they offer fifty-seven varieties of apples, including Sierra Beauty, another of my favorites, crisp with a hint of sweetness; Ashmead's Kernel, an old russet with sugary yellow flesh; and Spitzenburg, Thomas Jefferson's favorite apple. But they kept lots of Golden Delicious.

I never really liked Golden Delicious apples and couldn't understand their popularity, both here and in French pâtisseries, until I tasted one from the Apple Farm. I don't know what makes the difference—whether they are picked at just the right moment, or farmed just so, or some magic is involved—but the Golden Delicious apples from the Apple Farm are not like any others. Even their shape is different, conical instead of round. They have a slight green tinge at the beginning of their season, which changes to a pale yellow as the picking goes on—never the deep yellow, rubbery, stored-too-long globes found in supermarkets in January. They are fresh and juicy; the flesh breaks cleanly with each bite.

I'm glad that I don't have to name a definitive favorite apple. I can love them all as they come into season, savoring the late fruit as long as possible, and then do without from March until the first Gravensteins appear again. I admit that I'm an apple snob and will eat out-of-season supermarket apples only in an emergency—and never a Red Delicious.

I didn't have the luxury to be so picky when I had a bakery. Apples are a bakery's workhorse fruit. They fill in during the months when other fresh fruits aren't available. We used Golden Delicious, and sometimes Granny Smiths, when I studied pastry at Lenôtre's school in France, and in the beginning I blindly followed that example, preferring the Grannys for their tartness. They were always available. Then I discovered the Apple

Farm, and the seasonal nature of the apple struck home.

We made tarts from Gravensteins, one of the first apples to ripen. Apple tarts are the French equivalent of American apple pie. It takes three medium-size apples to make a nine-inch tart. First we peeled them, cut them in half, and scooped out the cores with a melon baller. Then we put them cut side down on the work counter and sliced them very thinly with a paring knife, keeping the slices in each half together. Shallow tart pans lined with dough and almond cream waited. We picked up an apple half and, as though dealing a deck of cards, carefully laid the slices on the almond cream inside the perimeter, overlapping them slightly. We made another circle inside the first one. Then we covered the center with a tight circle of small slices, like a flower. We gently brushed the sliced apples with apricot glaze, trying not to disturb their symmetry, then slid them into the oven. We baked them until the apples and crust were golden. Another brush with the glaze, and they were finished. The first thing I noticed was the difference in the way the apples colored in the oven. Granny Smiths always retained their raw pallor, no matter how long they baked. The sugars in the Gravensteins caramelized slightly in the oven, making them irresistible. And they tasted so much better. I looked forward to each apple variety as it ripened, and carted boxes from the Anderson Valley to the bakery.

In November, we filled tart pans lined with dough with roughly chopped apples (by then we had Sierra Beauties) and cranberries, poured an egg custard over the fruit, and baked it in the oven, a dessert more rustic than the apple tart. Again, the quality of the apples made this pastry so much better. It was only when all the local apples were gone that I gritted my teeth and resorted to Granny Smiths.

A few years ago, Karen's parents, Sally and Don Schmitt, retired from their restaurant, the French Laundry, in the Napa Valley, and joined Karen and Tim at the Apple Farm. But sitting in rocking chairs on the deck wasn't what they had in mind. They overhauled one of the original buildings, turning it into a welcoming kitchen where Sally gives cooking classes.

Sally likes to sauté peeled slices of Golden Delicious apples (one apple per person) in plenty of butter, then season them with salt and liberal grindings from a pepper mill. She serves them as a side dish with pork tenderloin, deglazing the pan with apple cider. This year, for the first time, she made peppered apples with Pink Pearls, their brilliant color adding another dimension to the dish. Nothing could be simpler than applesauce—slowly cooking a pot of peeled and cored, sliced apples with a little sugar until the apple's juice evaporates and the fruit's texture softens. Sally takes this comfort food one step further by adding butter and fresh thyme leaves, the herb bringing out the sweetness of the apples.

In addition to teaching classes, Sally puts up hundreds of jars of chutney and preserves that are for sale next to the fresh apples at their farm stand. And if a customer wants a tree of her own, there are some for sale, propagated by Nick King in nearby Point Arena, clustered near an upright at one end of the stand.

Nick King's distant uncles, the Lewelling brothers, left Iowa in 1847, their Conestogas so laden with fruit trees that they couldn't keep up with the wagon trains. The food writer Waverley Root credits them, along with William Meek, with starting commercial apple growing in the Pacific Northwest. Nick didn't know about this heritage when a college counselor advised him that his real calling was as a farmer; it took him ten more years to start the Garcia River Nursery. The business was well established when Nick's sister, tracing the family genealogy, made the connection.

I met Nick last year at the Boonville Farmers' Market. He had his present-day Conestoga, a black pickup, loaded with young apple trees for sale. To entice customers, he offered samplings of apples that the trees would eventually bear. I tasted a Cinnamon Spice, a tree of unknown origin found in Bolinas, California. It took a few chews for the cinnamon taste to emerge, but it was there, as if the apple had been sprinkled with cinnamon sugar. He also had Macouns, a cross of a McIntosh and a Jersey Black, that I thought had a fuller flavor than a plain McIntosh. The trees were healthy specimens, but I didn't have room for another in my orchard.

I drove over from the Anderson Valley one day in May to visit him. I knew that he was out in the country when his directions included mile markers instead of street names. The road out of Point Arena descends slowly to the valley etched by the Garcia River. His nursery is at the end of a dirt road on a flat, fertile plain close to the river. He pulled off his safety glasses and turned off the weed cutter when I pulled up. We stood in the sunshine among forty or fifty rows of small, grafted trees as we talked.

When he moved here with his family in the late 1960s, the land was an old farm where there were some apple trees, old varieties not usually seen. He started grafting the old trees to preserve them, then found interesting trees on other farms and propagated them as well. He realized he had a nursery business on his hands and started selling trees.

I told him about my small orchard and about the dilemma I faced last year when my Pink Pearl tree fruited for the first time. Although I had peeled and baked hundreds of apples at the bakery, I was in a quandary over when to pick the fruit—I didn't know when it was ripe. "You have to look at the seeds," he said. "They're white when the apples are developing but get darker, not necessarily black, but darker, when the apples are ripe."

When I asked Nick to name his favorite apple, his brow furrowed in concentration, and he looked into the distance for several seconds. "I'd have to say the Baldwin," he answered, extending his arms to a nearby tree as if he was about to embrace it. "The tree comes on so late, I almost forget about it every year. Then in November, sometimes December, it waves and says 'Hello, here I am.' It just pumps out fruit. The apples are so crisp that they crack when you bite them. It's a good tree for home gardens. People can buy apples in the early fall, then eat the Baldwins when the rest are gone," he said, echoing my belief that apples indeed have a season.

As I left, I noticed a completely rusted piece of equipment, not resembling modern farm machinery but tall and graceful, like a giant spider, beside a precariously listing barn. When I asked Nick what it was, he replied, "That's a horse-drawn road grader." I bet his uncles would have put it to good use.

Apple Tart with Almond Cream

An apple tart is one of life's simple pleasures. Many old-fashioned apple varieties don't travel well but are often superior in taste and texture. Seek out locally grown apples where you live; better yet, plant a few trees if you have room.

ONE 9-INCH TART, 8 SERVINGS

The tart dough

> *12 tablespoons (6 ounces) unsalted butter at room temperature*
> *½ cup (3½ ounces) granulated sugar*
> *1 extra-large egg*
> *½ teaspoon vanilla extract*
> *1¾ cups (8¾ ounces) unbleached all-purpose flour*

The almond cream

> *8 tablespoons (4 ounces) unsalted butter at room temperature*
> *Generous ¾ cup (4 ounces) unsifted powdered sugar*
> *¾ cup (4 ounces) blanched almonds, finely chopped, but not to a powder*
> *2 tablespoons unbleached all-purpose flour*
> *2 extra-large eggs at room temperature*
> *1 tablespoon dark Jamaican rum, preferably Myers's*

The apples and glaze

> *3 medium apples (1 pound), firm and tart*
> *Apricot glaze, made by heating ⅓ cup apricot preserves with 2 tablespoons water, then pushing it through a sieve*

Make the tart dough

Place the butter in the bowl of a heavy-duty mixer. Beat with the paddle at medium speed until it is creamy. Add the sugar and beat until light and fluffy. In a separate bowl, beat the egg and vanilla together with a fork. With the mixer running, add the egg. Scrape the bowl and mix well. Add the flour all at once, and mix until it is just incorporated.

Remove the dough from the bowl, flatten it to a disk 1 inch thick on a piece of plastic wrap, cover it with more plastic wrap, and refrigerate it for 1 hour, or up to 3 days. The dough can also be frozen, tightly wrapped, for 1 month.

Make the almond cream

Beat the butter with a paddle at medium speed in the bowl of a heavy-duty mixer until it is creamy. Add the sugar, almonds, and flour and beat until everything is well combined. In a separate bowl, beat the eggs with the rum. With the mixer running, dribble the egg and rum into the mixing bowl. If the mixture starts to curdle, switch to a whisk and beat until it looks smooth again. Refrigerate the cream if not using it immediately.

Assemble and bake the tart

Preheat the oven to 375°F.

Remove the dough from the refrigerator and roll it into a disk ⅛ inch thick on a lightly floured work surface. If the dough cracks and resists rolling, it is too cold. Let it warm a little, or pound it with a rolling pin, then proceed. Transfer the dough to a fluted 9-inch tart pan that has a removable bottom and is 1 inch deep. Gently ease the dough into the bottom and up the sides of the pan. Run the rolling pin over the top edges of the pan to cut the dough. Chill it in the freezer while you prepare the apples.

Peel the apples. Cut them into halves from top to bottom. Remove the cores with a melon baller. Put them, cut side down, on a work surface. Cut straight down through the apple, making very thin slices, about ¹⁄₁₆ inch thick, trying to keep the slices together.

Spoon the almond cream into the tart shell, and smooth it evenly with a spatula. Pick up half an apple and hold it in one hand. With your other hand, "deal" the slices like a deck of cards, placing them one at a time inside the perimeter, overlapping them slightly. Make another circle inside the first one, overlapping the first by half. Cover the center of the tart with a third circle. This will look like too many apples, but they cook down, and the baked tart will look just right. Gently brush the apples with the glaze, trying not to disturb their symmetry.

Put the tart in the middle shelf of the oven and bake until the almond cream is set and the apples are browned, 40 to 45 minutes.

Cool the tart in the pan, then transfer it to a serving platter, and brush with more apricot glaze. Refrigerate if not serving immediately.

FRESH APPLE SALSA

from the Apple Farm

Thanks to Sally Schmitt and Karen Bates for this recipe. This refreshing salsa is easy to make and goes well with grilled chicken or halibut or roast pork. It is best served the day it is made.

I like jalapeño and Anaheim chiles in this salsa. If you like it hotter, use a serrano chile instead of the jalapeño. Be careful not to rub your eyes while handling hot chiles. If you are particularly sensitive to their oil, wear rubber gloves.

4 TO 6 SERVINGS

    2 tart apples, locally grown if possible
    ¼ cup lime juice
    1 fresh jalapeño chile
    1 fresh Anaheim chile
    ½ medium onion, finely chopped
    Handful cilantro, roughly chopped
    ½ cup (2 ounces) walnuts, coarsely chopped and lightly toasted
    2 tablespoons peeled and finely slivered fresh ginger
    ¼ teaspoon salt

Remove the cores from the apples, but don't peel them, and cut into ¼-inch cubes.

Toss the apple pieces with the lime juice and set aside.

Cut the chiles in half lengthwise and remove the seeds and white ribs. Slice them thinly and add them to the apples. Add the onion, cilantro, walnuts, ginger, and salt, and mix everything together.

Apples Baked in Pastry

About six years ago, while perusing the selection at a used book store, I saw a small volume called *Cuisine Normande*. It contained recipes using the bounty of that region of France—butter, cream, and cider. I was intrigued by the unusual preparation of a pastry dough that enveloped ripe pears—white wine beaten into butter, then combined with the dry ingredients. I bought the book, and we tried the recipe at the bakery. We sold many of those pastry-wrapped pears at the Saturday farmers' market. This is my version using apples.

6 SERVINGS

The pastry

    2 tablespoons granulated sugar
    2 cups (10 ounces) unbleached all-purpose flour
    16 tablespoons (8 ounces) unsalted butter at room temperature
    ½ cup (4 ounces) dry white wine

The apples

    6 medium-size flavorful, firm apples
    ½ cup (3½ ounces) granulated sugar
    1 teaspoon ground cinnamon
    Egg wash: 1 extra-large egg beaten with 2 tablespoons water

Make the pastry

Sift the sugar and the flour together and set aside.

Put the butter in the bowl of a heavy-duty mixer. Using the paddle and with the mixer on medium speed, add the wine in small quantities, waiting until each addition is absorbed before continuing. Add the flour mixture all at once to the butter. Mix until the dough is just combined. Turn it out onto a floured work surface and knead it a few turns. Flatten it into a disk, wrap it in plastic, and refrigerate it for at least 2 hours, or up to 4 days.

Wrap and bake the apples

Preheat the oven to 400°F.

Peel the apples, but leave the stems and cores intact. Mix the sugar and cinnamon together.

Roll out the pastry on a floured work surface to a thickness of ⅛ inch. Cut a strip slightly larger than the height of an apple and long enough to wrap around its circumference. Roll the apple in the cinnamon sugar, then wrap the pastry strip around it, pleating it around the stem to make it fit. Fold the pastry together at the bottom of the apple, trimming any excess. Either push the dough together or use a moistened finger to seal the seams. This is a rustic dessert; the pastry covering doesn't have to look perfect. Stand the finished apple on a parchment-lined baking pan. Wrap the other apples and put them on the baking pan. Cut "leaves" from the dough scraps and attach them to the tops of the apples.

Brush the apples with the egg wash, and sprinkle them with some of the cinnamon/sugar mixture.

Bake the apples in the middle of the oven until the pastry is browned and the apples are bubbling and soft when poked with a skewer, about 40 minutes. Serve warm or at room temperature.

Warm Cabbage Salad with Apples

A friend recently ordered this salad at 231 Ellsworth Restaurant in San Mateo. When he offered me a taste, I wished I had ordered it too. Thanks to Rod Boyd, the chef, for sharing his recipe. The addition of the apples was my idea.

4 SERVINGS AS A FIRST COURSE

The vinaigrette
> *1 tablespoon champagne wine vinegar, 7% acidity*
> *½ clove garlic, minced*
> *2 tablespoons (1 ounce) extra-virgin olive oil*
> *2 tablespoons (1 ounce) canola oil*
> *Salt and pepper to taste*
> *1 tablespoon (1 ounce) blue cheese, crumbled*

The croutons
> *4 slices rustic bread*
> *½ clove garlic*
> *Extra-virgin olive oil*

The salad
> *¼ pound thick-sliced bacon from the butcher, cut crosswise into*
> * ¼-inch strips*
> *½ head (1 pound) green cabbage, cored and thinly sliced*
> *2 (¾ pound) tasty autumn apples, peeled, cored, and thinly sliced*

Make the vinaigrette

Put the vinegar and garlic into a small bowl. Drizzle in the oils, whisking constantly. Add salt and pepper to taste. Stir in the cheese. Set the vinaigrette aside.

Make the croutons

Toast the bread. While it is warm, rub one side of each piece with the cut face of the garlic. Drizzle olive oil over the slices.

Make the salad

Cook the bacon in a 12-inch skillet or wok. When it is crisp, drain the fat from the pan. Add the cabbage and apples. Cook them, tossing the pan, until they are warm and just starting to soften, a few minutes. They should still be crunchy. Add the vinaigrette and stir everything together. Serve the salad on warm plates with a crouton on top.

An Excuse for a Lunch

A CAPACITY CROWD MINGLED AMONG WHITE-CLOTHED TABLES in the Palace of Fine Arts, an old pavilion that was part of the Pan-American Exhibition earlier in the century. Some tables held pâtés, others bread and cheese, but the majority were covered with bottles of Beaujolais Nouveau, jetted in by their French producers on the third Thursday of November, the traditional day of the wine's release in France. It was the first Beaujolais Nouveau celebration in San Francisco, organized by the French-American Chamber of Commerce and chaired by my husband, Sidney. The party atmosphere that prevails in French bars and restaurants on that day had spread to San Francisco, and the revelers came, despite the driving rain. Speeches were made, raffle prizes were distributed, and all the wine was drunk.

Because that first celebration many years ago was such a success, it has been repeated year after year. It moved from the cramped quarters of the Palace of Fine Arts to larger venues, then to cavernous halls. More people came; live music was added. As it expanded, it lost its charm for us, and we stopped going.

One evening several years ago, we were reminiscing with friends about the early Beaujolais festivals and feeling nostalgic for the way we remembered them, as parties among friends. Then one of the group suggested a way to recapture the fun of the early events. "Let's have a Beaujolais Nouveau lunch for some of the people who were part of the first one," he said. He and his wife volunteered their house. The date was set—the Friday after the release of the wine. I felt as though I were playing hooky from school. We gathered in our friends' kitchen until everyone arrived. Although it wasn't planned, each person brought a different bottle of Beaujolais. Most of them were made in the *nouveau* style, a technique called carbonic maceration, where whole clusters of grapes undergo a special fermentation in an oxygen-starved atmosphere. This unique style of fermentation evidently began in the nineteenth century when the wine completed its fermentation in casks as it traveled to Lyon, a large city south of the wine-growing region. The method produces a young, fruity wine, which can be drunk after two months, unlike other wines, which require a longer rest from vine to table. All the wine is made from one grape variety, Gamay Noir à Jus Blanc, which is different from the Napa Gamay (now called Valdiguié) and Gamay Beaujolais grown in California.

It is the perfect quaffing wine to accompany bistro food. There are wine bars in Paris that specialize in Beaujolais—raucous places where people sit at cramped tables eating quiche Lorraine and plates of charcuterie while drinking Beaujolais decanted from barrels. To me, the wine is associated with laughter and unpretentious meals. It is not a wine for aging or intense discussion, although there are ten districts, called *crus*, that produce superior wines. These will keep longer, but should be drunk within three years.

We lined up the bottles on the counter. One was a Beaujolais Nouveau from the Napa Valley, a wine in a special category because of the confusion that reigns over the variety of grapes used. Our friends brought out every wineglass they owned, enough so that each person had one for each wine.

Henri Lapuyade arrived, carrying a large box holding a variety of his pâtés. He had been at the first Beaujolais festival at the Palace of Fine Arts, serving slabs of pâté on slices of baguette. A generous man, he frequently offers samples at fund-raising events in the Bay Area. Mr. "Parlez-vous Pâté?" first introduced French pâtés and sausages to San Franciscans in 1960 when he opened a small meat market and charcuterie on Russian Hill with a partner, Marcel Moura. I remember making a trek to his shop many years ago for sausages to put in a cassoulet. He eventually outgrew that space and moved to a larger production space in South San Francisco. Now Marcel et Henri Charcuterie Française makes and ships astounding quantities of pâtés throughout this country and as far away as Hong Kong.

We assembled at the dining room table. A squadron of glasses stood at the ready in front of each person. Bottles covered the middle of the table. We started with Henri's pâtés, and platters of thinly sliced ham, rounds of salamis, and hard-to-find smoked meats. Next were ducks roasted in a very hot oven and carved at the table. A palate cleanser of a *frisée* salad followed. Then a cheese platter appeared, a young goat cheese from France, a crumbly Stilton, and an English cheddar. We ate them with slices of walnut bread that I had baked. A chocolate chestnut cake brought the meal to a close.

We had succeeded. Celebrating the Beaujolais Nouveau was fun again. It was the beginning of a new tradition. Before we left that day, Sidney's business partner and his wife invited everyone to their house for the second annual Beaujolais Nouveau lunch to be held the Friday after the wine was released the following year. I've never planned anything so far in advance. I didn't even have a calendar for the next year.

The next November we drove, we met, and we ate again. These lunches were starting to feel like training camp for Thanksgiving dinner. At the close of that lunch, Henri invited all of us to tour his plant. We met there the following February, giving everyone time to recover from any possible holiday excesses.

It's not a large space, considering the amount of meat that is prepared. Just inside the door is an office for the USDA inspector, who is there every day. We donned white paper hats and followed Henri around. The kitchen is a meat lover's dream. Every part of the pig is put to use. Huge pans of pork—some ground, some sliced—sat on stainless tables. But pork isn't the exclusive ingredient. Veal, duck, chicken, turkey, venison, rabbit, and livers, lots of livers, are also made into pâtés—some in pastry crusts or infused with Cognac, others embellished with truffles, pistachios, prunes, or juniper berries. Huge ovens bake filled terrines on heavy trays. Even larger refrigerators and freezers cool and preserve the contents. Expensive, sophisticated equipment vacuum-wraps the pâtés for distribution.

Standing in the middle of the kitchen, the air heavy with cooking meat, I could almost feel the pâté entering my body through osmosis.

All this meat was making us ravenous. Henri gave everyone a large box full of samples. Each contained several fat slices of different pâtés and two kinds of sausages: spicy merguez, made from lamb, and blood sausages. I told Sidney he could have the blood sausages. Then Henri took us all to lunch at the nearby Basque Cultural Center, where he is a founding member.

Sidney and I hosted the third Beaujolais Nouveau lunch. Henri Lapuyade was out of town, so seven of us hurried to complete our work by 1:00 P.M. Our friend who had sparked the idea for these gatherings arrived last, working his car phone all the way to our front door. As punishment, we made him recite all ten *crus* of Beaujolais before he could have a glass of wine. Sidney and another friend who had worked at the French-American Chamber wore fancy silver *tastevins*, tasting cups with handles on green silk ropes that hang around the neck. They received them when they were inducted into the *Compagnons du Beaujolais*, a wine fraternity sponsored by Beaujolais producers, in recognition of their work with the Beaujolais Nouveau events. The rest of us resorted to wine glasses. The lunch began with a *salade Beaujolaise*, a traditional mix of *frisée*, croutons, and *lardons* made from pancetta, all moistened with a mustard vinaigrette and topped with a poached egg. Cabbage bundles, stuffed with pork, chestnuts, and spices and then cooked slowly until the cabbage is tender and tastes of the stuffing, followed. A cheese course helped us drink the last of the wine, then a cranberry tart and coffee ended the meal. The other member of the *Compagnons*, who is a reluctant chef, agreed to be hostess the next time. She was relieved when those of us who love to cook promised to help.

Salade Beaujolaise

The only break with tradition in this version of *salade Beaujolaise* is the use of pancetta, the peppery, rolled Italian bacon, instead of regular smoked bacon; it adds a little zest to the salad. Look for small heads of *frisée*; the larger ones will be tough.

8 SERVINGS

The vinaigrette

1 teaspoon Dijon-style mustard
2 tablespoons red wine vinegar, 7% acidity
½ cup (4 ounces) extra-virgin olive oil
Salt and pepper

The salad

2 heads frisée, *washed and torn into manageable pieces*
4 pieces good white bread, cut into cubes and toasted
½ pound pancetta, cut into cubes, fried, and drained
8 medium eggs

Make the vinaigrette

Mix the mustard and the vinegar together in a small bowl with a fork. Add the olive oil, a few drops at a time, while continuing to mix. The vinaigrette should start to emulsify. If it doesn't, stop adding oil and mix vigorously until it does. Mix in the remainder of the oil. Salt and pepper lightly. More can be added after tasting the *frisée* once it has been dressed.

Make the salad and poach the eggs

Place the *frisée*, bread, and fried pancetta in a large bowl. Pour the vinaigrette over the salad and toss, coating everything well. Taste for salt and pepper. Mound the salad on 8 serving plates.

Choose a skillet that will hold 4 eggs, and fill it with water. (Or use two skillets and poach all the eggs at once.) Add a teaspoon of vinegar to the water. Bring the water to a simmer. Carefully crack 4 eggs into the water and cook them until the whites are opaque. Don't let the water boil. Remove the eggs with a slotted spoon and set them on a kitchen towel to drain. Poach the remaining eggs and drain them as well. The eggs can be cooked before the salad is dressed; they don't have to be hot when served. Gently top each salad with an egg. Salt and pepper the eggs and serve.

STUFFED CABBAGE BUNDLES WITH CHESTNUTS

Rustic dishes made with cabbage permeate the French countryside, and chestnuts are often added to give a deeper flavor. These bundles of cabbage, resting on a bed of carrots and onions, are hearty, filling fare, perfect for the cold winter months. Serve these with a crusty bread to hungry people.

The cabbage leaves can be prepared a day ahead and refrigerated. Fill them with the stuffing and cook them the next day. Although this dish can be cooked in a moderate oven, simmering it on top of the stove makes it easier to check occasionally.

If you use shelled chestnuts, buy the vacuum-packed nuts from France, available in specialty food stores. They are superior to canned nuts.

ABOUT 25 ROLLS, 6 SERVINGS

The stuffing
> 1 pound in-the-shell chestnuts, or ½ pound shelled chestnuts
> 2 tablespoons mild-flavored vegetable oil
> 1 medium onion, peeled and finely chopped
> 2 cloves garlic, finely chopped
> 1 pound ground pork
> ½ pound bacon, diced
> 1½ teaspoons dried thyme
> Generous ¼ teaspoon each nutmeg, cloves, ginger, and black pepper
> 1½ teaspoons salt

The cabbage
> 1 large head green cabbage (about 1 pound)
> 2 tablespoons vegetable oil
> 3 medium carrots, peeled and sliced
> 1 medium onion, coarsely chopped
> 2 cups water

Make the stuffing

If using chestnuts in the shell, make a cross with a sharp knife in the flat side of each one. Roast them in a 400°F oven until the cut shells pull away from the nuts. Remove from the oven and cover with a kitchen towel to keep them hot. As soon as you can handle them, peel away the outer shell and the papery skin underneath. Work with a few at a time, keeping the rest in the roasting pan. If they cool completely, they will be impossible to shell. If this happens, put them back in the oven for a few minutes, then try again.

Roughly chop the peeled nuts (either fresh or purchased), and set aside.

Heat the oil in a small skillet. Add the onion and garlic and cook until soft but not browned, about 10 minutes. Cool to room temperature.

In a large bowl, mix together the chestnuts, pork, bacon, thyme, spices, and salt. Add the cooked onion and garlic and mix well. Cook a small patty in the skillet used for the onion and garlic and taste for seasoning. Adjust it if needed.

Prepare the cabbage

Bring a large pot of salted water to a boil. Put the cabbage upside down on a work surface and cut out the core. Fill a large bowl with cold water. Place the cabbage, top side up, in the boiling water. As the outside leaves separate from the head, remove them, using tongs, to the bowl of cold water. When only the small inner leaves remain, remove them from the boiling water. Chop these small leaves coarsely and set aside.

Drain the large cabbage leaves. Arrange them with the thick portion that attached to the core facing you, concave side up. Place a generous portion of stuffing in the middle of each leaf, fold the sides over the stuffing, then fold up the end facing you. Fold the top of the leaf down to make a rectangular bundle. The amount of stuffing used will vary with the size of the cabbage leaves. Don't worry if you don't use it all.

Cook the cabbage bundles

Use a large, heavy, nonreactive pot that will hold the bundles in two layers. Heat the oil and cook the carrots and onion until they are soft but not browned. Turn off the heat. Strew the chopped inner cabbage leaves over the other vegetables. Sprinkle any leftover stuffing over the chopped cabbage. Put the bundles in the pot, seam side down, and add the water. Bring to a simmer, cover, and cook until the cabbage is soft, about 1½ hours.

Serve the bundles on warm plates, with a spoonful of cooking juices to moisten each serving.

CRANBERRY-ORANGE TART

The first cranberries in the markets herald the start of the winter holidays, and this tart complements any festive menu, especially a lunch celebrating the Beaujolais Nouveau wine.

Prepare the orange slices the day before you bake the tart.

ONE 9-INCH TART, 8 SERVINGS

The orange slices

> ½ orange
> ⅔ cup (5 ounces) water
> ⅓ cup (2½ ounces) granulated sugar

The tart dough

> 12 tablespoons (6 ounces) unsalted butter at room temperature
> ½ cup (3½ ounces) granulated sugar
> 1 extra-large egg
> ½ teaspoon vanilla extract
> 1¾ cups (8¾ ounces) unbleached all-purpose flour

The cranberry-orange filling and apricot glaze

> 18 ounces (1½ packages) fresh cranberries (reserve 16 of the remaining berries for decoration)
> ¾ cup (6 ounces) water
> 1 cup (7 ounces) granulated sugar
> Apricot glaze made by heating ⅓ cup apricot preserves with 2 tablespoons water, then pushing it through a sieve

Prepare the orange slices

Only half of the orange is needed. Cut it into thin slices, discarding any seeds. Place the slices in a small bowl. Bring the water and sugar to a boil, stirring to dissolve the sugar. Pour the syrup over the orange slices. Cover and refrigerate overnight, or up to a week.

Make the tart dough

Put the butter in the bowl of a heavy-duty mixer. Beat it with the paddle until creamy. Add the sugar and beat until the mixture is light and fluffy. In a separate bowl, beat the egg and vanilla together with a fork. With the mixer running, add the egg. Scrape the bowl and mix well. Add the flour all at once and mix until it is just incorporated. Remove the dough from the bowl, flatten it to a thickness of ½ inch on a piece of plastic wrap, cover it with more plastic wrap, and refrigerate for 1 hour, or up to 3 days. The dough can also be frozen, tightly wrapped, for 1 month.

Make the filling

Combine the cranberries, water, and sugar in a saucepan and cook until the berries "pop" and the mixture thickens. Some of the berries should hold their shape. Don't cook them to a purée. Drain the orange slices and chop them finely. Stir into the cranberries. The filling can be made up to 5 days ahead and kept refrigerated.

Bake the tart

Preheat the oven to 375°F.

Remove the dough from the refrigerator and roll it into a disk ⅛ inch thick on a lightly floured work surface. If the dough cracks and resists rolling, it is too cold. Let it warm a little, or pound it with a rolling pin, then proceed. Transfer the dough to a fluted 9-inch tart pan that has a removable bottom and is 1 inch deep. Gently ease the dough into the bottom and up the sides of the pan. Run the rolling pin over the top edges of the pan to cut the dough. Chill it in the freezer for 10 minutes. Cover the dough with parchment paper, pressing it into the bottom edge. Fill the pan with rice or dried beans and bake it until the sides are lightly browned, about 10 minutes. Remove the beans and parchment paper, and return the pan to the oven until the bottom is set, another 5 minutes.

Spoon the filling into the partially baked shell, return it to the oven, and bake the tart until the filling is bubbling and the crust browned, 20 minutes. Cool on a rack.

Transfer the tart from the pan to a serving dish. Brush with apricot glaze. Coat 16 of the remaining whole cranberries in sugar by rolling the raw, damp berries in granulated sugar, then place them around the outside border of the tart.

Uncommon Citrus

MOST PEOPLE IN THIS COUNTRY KNOW ORANGES. Even if they have never seen an orange on a tree, they surely have drunk orange juice, either from a carton or from a glass filled with reconstituted frozen concentrate—three cans of water shaken with one can of frozen orange slush. Oranges are so prevalent in this country, with vast groves of trees in California and Florida, that when John McPhee started writing an article about them he ended up with enough material for a book. Grapefruits and lemons aren't far behind oranges in recognition and popularity.

But what about the lesser-known citrus fruits, the ones not grown acre after acre to fill production and marketing schemes? Take citrons, for example. I only knew them as green horrors baked into commercial fruitcakes until a baker strode into the bakery one day clutching a brown paper bag. The mischievous look on her face told us it contained something special. She upended the bag. Odd-looking lemons, very fragrant, more oblong than round, with bumpy skin, tumbled onto the wooden table. We looked at her quizzically. "Citrons," she pronounced. "Fresh citrons—really?" I asked. None of us had ever seen a fresh citron. I cut one in half. The inside revealed the characteristic thick pith under the peel, much thicker than that of other citrus fruits, and a small, fleshy interior. What a find.

One of the college students who delivered bread ambled over to see what was causing the flurry. "Oh, they look just like the lemons that grow on a tree in my backyard," he said. Exotic citrons growing in a San Francisco backyard? I asked him to bring some to the bakery. The next day he arrived with a cardboard box full. His family didn't like them; they were glad to see them go. They certainly looked the same—pebbled skin with thick pith. After much thought about what to do with them, we made them into marmalade, a much better fate than dyeing them green for fruitcakes. The customers were curious about the sparkling jars on the retail counter. "What's in the jars?" they asked. "Citron marmalade," we answered. "What does it taste like?" "Like lemons, only better," we told them. The jars didn't last long. A few years later, when the tree's owner no longer worked at the bakery, I thought of it one overcast January afternoon. I called him and negotiated a trade—citrons for pastry.

Evidently, citrons were more familiar a long time ago. *The Roman Cookery of Apicius*, a manuscript from the fourth century A.D., includes a recipe for a meat ragout with citron. I haven't seen anything like it on today's San Francisco restaurant menus, but it sounds tasty. Although citrons were included in the first citrus plantings in Florida in the sixteenth century, oranges and grapefruits are now the dominant citrus crops there. Citrons have one advantage over the other citrus—because of their thick skin, they make the best candied peel, perfect baked into a Dresden stollen for the holidays.

One special variety of citron, although its peel can also be candied, is better suited to being piled in a bowl and used as a centerpiece. These citrons are the anthropomorphic "Buddha's Hand." The end that attaches to the tree is solid, but about two inches down the fruit separates into finger-like projections that curl together at the end. It looks as if it has the uncanny ability to open and close. I have never seen a Buddha's Hand tree, but it must be an extraordinary sight: little hands dangling from leafed branches.

There is another citrus that is a newborn in comparison to the centuries-old citron. It's the Meyer lemon, and Californians like to claim it as their own. It's certainly more prevalent than the citron, and it's more user-friendly. Two blocks from my house, the top of a Meyer lemon tree peeks over a tall fence. It is laden with fruit most of the year. I have two friends living in the city who bring me bags of Meyer lemons from their very productive trees. My eight-year-old tree is another story. When I bought it, I planted it in a sawed-off wine barrel. After three years, the only lemon on it was the small metal disk attached to its base that identified it as an

Improved Meyer Lemon. I moved it to the garden. I fertilized it. I tried more water, then less water. Finally, last year it produced a few lemons. I used them judiciously. This year, it was slightly more forthcoming, but I still treat its fruit like precious gems, carefully calculating how to use them.

The Meyer lemon is a hybrid, with a lemon and a mandarin orange for parents. It appeared in California at the beginning of the century, brought here from China by Frank Meyer, an American gardener. It became a backyard tree, grown for its fruit as well as for its ornamental value. In the 1940s the trees developed a bad reputation; they were found to harbor a virus that threatened California's entire citrus production, so most were destroyed. But thanks to researchers at the University of California at Riverside, the virus-free Improved Meyer was developed, so now they're back, although still not prevalent outside California. Few folks in Florida know them.

From January to April, when the crop is at its peak, Meyer lemons show up in sweet and savory dishes on Bay Area restaurant menus—in vinaigrette and sorbet, splashed on grilled fish and cooked with eggs in lemon curd. Their popularity is usually attributed to Alice Waters, who pioneered their use during the early days of her restaurant, Chez Panisse. Home cooks use them too, finding them in their backyards, in produce stores, or at farmers' markets. They are sweeter than the more common Eureka and Lisbon lemon varieties and are set apart by their floral aroma. The aroma can be deceiving, enticing the unsuspecting to eat them like oranges. But their strong lemon taste comes through with the first bite.

Although I love citrons for baking, and will reach for a Meyer lemon instead of an Eureka if they're available, blood oranges are my favorite obscure citrus fruit. I was living in Brussels the first time I saw blood oranges. I brought them home in a net sack that I had purchased at a small grocery store. From the outside, they looked like regular oranges, perhaps a bit more colored. I cut one open and stared at it in astonishment. The orange flesh was marbled dark red, almost burgundy. I couldn't decide if it was diseased or had been injected to improve its color. I cut open another. It looked the same. Dye, I decided, and threw them out. A few days later,

I was in a produce store where the proprietor was very proud of his pristine fruit. Next to a pile of oranges was one that had been cut in half, revealing the same marbled color of the bunch I had discarded. I asked the owner about them. He explained that they were the first crop of the highly regarded blood oranges from Italy. I nodded in what I hoped was a knowing fashion, and bought a few. This time I took them home, cut into one, and tasted it. Its taste wasn't straightforward, like a good California navel, but more complex—sweetness wrapped up in a distinct raspberry flavor, like eating a bowl of berries swimming in orange juice.

When we returned to San Francisco, there wasn't a blood orange in sight. Although a third of all oranges eaten in the Mediterranean region of Europe are blood oranges, they were still an oddity here. A few years later, some trickled into the markets in January. I decided to investigate. There are three varieties: Moro and Tarocco, both Italian; and Sanguinelli, from Spain. I was curious about which variety the local farmers grew.

I wrote down the name of the packing company stamped on a box of blood oranges in a market.

After speaking with several people who claimed never to have seen blood oranges, I finally was given the number of someone who was said to carry them. I dialed the phone and, when a man answered, I explained why I was calling.

"Yeah, we have blood oranges."

"Which variety are they?"

"Moro."

"How long have you had them?"

"About ten years." Not very talkative, I thought.

"Have they been a good seller for you?"

"They're a little hard to sell. The problem is, everybody has a little, not a lot. If the chains can't put them in all their stores, they won't buy them, so we have to find smaller markets."

"I've read that their color is unpredictable, making them harder to market. Is that your experience?"

"Well, this year, the outside of the fruit looks like a navel. They're real bloody inside, but the housewife doesn't know that. The produce people have to cut them open so customers can see the inside. But they don't always do that."

"So they need a stronger sales pitch than regular oranges," I said.

"Yeah, and that's not all. Another problem is that they're alternate bearing. One year is a heavy crop, with small fruit. The next year the crop is lighter, not as colored, and bigger. This year is a light year and they are humongous. So they're not as predictable as other fruits. We also grow more reliable crops, other citrus, table grapes, peaches, and some vegetables."

"Thanks for your help," I said as I ended the conversation.

I have tasted all three varieties. The Moro and the Sanguinelli tasted similar to me, although the Moro was more berrylike. The Taroccos that I sampled were lightly colored inside, with a spicy, almost bitter edge. I liked the Moros the best. Their raspberry flavor and deep color add a dramatic touch to salads and sauces. And a blood orange mousse is the perfect Valentine's Day dessert.

The blood oranges need a marketing professional and a clever public relations firm. Then more farmers might take a chance and plant the trees. Sometimes obscure fruit doesn't get the attention its complex taste deserves, especially when giant crops that are similar dominate the picture. Any baker will appreciate a fresh citron. A trip to San Francisco restaurants in the early spring should convert anyone to Meyer lemons. And anyone who likes oranges is sure to love blood oranges.

MEYER LEMON POUND CAKE

Fresh lemon juice and Meyer lemon zest that is soaked overnight in sugar syrup give this cake its distinctive taste.

Prepare the lemon zest ahead—at least one day, or up to one week, before baking.

ONE LOAF, 6 TO 8 SERVINGS

The lemon zest

> *4 medium Meyer lemons*
> *½ cup (4 ounces) water*
> *½ cup (3½ ounces) granulated sugar*

The cake

> *1¼ cups (6¼ ounces) unbleached all-purpose flour*
> *½ teaspoon baking powder*
> *10 tablespoons (5 ounces) unsalted butter at room temperature*
> *1 cup (7 ounces) granulated sugar*
> *2 extra-large eggs at room temperature*
> *⅓ cup (2½ ounces) Meyer lemon juice*

Prepare the lemon zest

Cut the zest from the lemons, leaving as much of the pith as possible on the fruit. Remove any pith still attached to the zest. A good way to do this is by scraping the zest with the dull side of a paring knife. Put the zest in a small container. Bring the water and sugar to a boil, stirring to dissolve the sugar. Pour the sugar syrup over the lemon zest. Cover and refrigerate overnight, or up to a week. Juice enough of the lemons to make ⅓ cup, and reserve for the cake.

Mix the batter and bake the cake

Preheat the oven to 350°F. Generously butter a 6-cup loaf pan.

Drain the lemon zest and chop finely.

Sift together the flour and baking powder and set aside. Beat the butter in the bowl of a heavy-duty mixer with the paddle until it is creamy. Add the sugar and beat until the mixture is fluffy. Break the eggs into a separate small bowl and beat them lightly with a fork. With the mixer running, add the eggs, a little at a time, waiting for each addition to become incorporated before adding more. Add the dry ingredients alternately with the lemon juice. Mix in the lemon zest. Pour the batter into the loaf pan and bake on the middle shelf of the oven until a skewer inserted into the middle comes out clean, about 1 hour. Cool the cake, then remove it from the pan.

Blood Orange Mousse Cake

Blood oranges bring a pink hue and a taste of raspberry to the mousse that is the body of this dessert. Cubes of *génoise* cake are folded into the mousse, and all is molded in a bowl. Serve it as dessert for a special Valentine's Day dinner.

The cake can be made up to 3 days ahead, then wrapped and refrigerated. The dessert needs to chill for at least 4 hours before unmolding, so make it the night before or the morning of the day it is served.

A candy thermometer is needed to make this dessert.

Use a stainless steel bowl or charlotte mold with a 6-cup capacity to mold the mousse. It's important that the bowl be metal so it can be heated for unmolding.

8 SERVINGS

The *génoise* cake

> 3 extra-large eggs
> ⅓ cup (2½ ounces) granulated sugar
> 2 tablespoons (1 ounce) unsalted butter
> ½ cup (2½ ounces) cake flour, sifted

The mousse

> ¼ cup egg whites (2 large) at room temperature
> 2 tablespoons granulated sugar
> 2 tablespoons water
> ½ cup (3½ ounces) granulated sugar
> 2 pounds blood oranges (6 or 7)
> 1 cup (8 ounces) heavy whipping cream
> 1 envelope (2½ teaspoons) unflavored gelatin

Make the *génoise*

Preheat the oven to 375°F.

Line the bottom of a 7 x 2½-inch cake pan with parchment paper.

Put the eggs and sugar in the bowl of a heavy-duty mixer, then put this bowl over a pan of simmering water. Whisk the mixture by hand until it reaches 140°F, about 3 minutes. Don't overheat it, or the eggs will scramble. Put the bowl on the mixer. Place the butter in a 1-quart bowl and set it over the simmering water to melt while you proceed.

Beat the egg mixture with a whisk at high speed until the mixture cools, becomes pale and thick, and almost triples in volume, 8 to 10 minutes. Remove the bowl from the mixer.

Sift half of the flour over the egg mixture and fold it in. (This will be the second time the flour is sifted.) Use a rubber spatula to fold, going to the bottom of the bowl in the center and coming up along the side. Rotate the bowl slightly after every fold. Repeat with the rest of the flour. Remove the butter bowl from the water. Fold about one-fifth of the egg mixture into the butter, then return this butter-enriched batter to the original bowl and fold it in.

Immediately pour the batter into the pan and place on the middle shelf of the oven.

Bake until the cake starts to pull away from the sides of the pan and the center just under the crust is baked, about 20 minutes. Cool the cake in its pan on a rack, then run a knife around the edges and remove it from the pan.

Make the mousse and assemble the dessert

First make a meringue. Place the egg whites and 1 tablespoon of the sugar in the bowl of a mixer. Start whisking at slow speed. Combine the water and ½ cup sugar in a small saucepan and bring to a boil, washing down any sugar crystals that collect on the sides of the pan with a wet brush. Using a candy thermometer, boil until the syrup reaches 240°F. Add the remaining tablespoon of sugar to the beating whites and turn the mixer speed to high. When the syrup reaches 250°F, take it from the heat and, with the mixer running, pour it into the egg whites. Aim for the side of the bowl, avoiding the whisk. Turn the speed to low and continue preparations for the mousse as the meringue cools to room temperature.

Only half of the cake is needed for this dessert. Cut it in half, wrap the unused portion in plastic wrap, and reserve. Cut the cake into 1-inch cubes.

Remove the zest from 3 of the oranges with a fine zester or use a knife, then finely chop the zest. Set 1 orange aside for garnish and juice the rest. There should be 1½ cups of juice.

Beat the whipping cream until soft peaks form, then fold it into the cooled meringue.

Put about a third of the juice in a small saucepan. Sprinkle the gelatin over the juice and wait until it softens. Heat until the gelatin dissolves. Stir this into the remaining juice.

Whisk a third of the cream/meringue mixture into the juice to thicken it, then fold in the rest of the cream/meringue and the orange zest. Fold in the cake cubes. Pour the mousse into a stainless 6-cup capacity bowl and smooth the top. Refrigerate until firm, at least 4 hours or overnight.

Unmold the dessert

Invert the bowl onto a plate. Warm it with a hot towel or a blowtorch. Remove the bowl and smooth the mousse with a small spatula. Thinly slice the reserved orange, then cut the slices in half. Press them cut side down into the mousse around the base and serve.

CITRUS SALAD WITH FENNEL

This is a salad of circles: shaved fennel, slices of peeled lemons and oranges, and red onions. Serve with crusty bread as a first course before roasted meat.

The fennel should be cut as thinly as possible. The best tool for doing this is a mandoline. If you don't have one, use a sharp knife or a fine slicing blade on a food processor. The citrus is too soft to cut on a mandoline; use a knife instead.

6 SERVINGS

1 fennel bulb, thinly sliced
½ red onion, thinly sliced
2 Meyer lemons, peel, pith, and seeds removed, thinly sliced
Salt and pepper
1 tablespoon Meyer lemon juice
3 tablespoons extra-virgin olive oil
2 blood oranges, peel, pith, and seeds removed, thinly sliced

Toss the fennel, onion, lemons, salt, and pepper with the lemon juice, then with the olive oil. Add the oranges last and lightly mix them in, so they don't discolor the rest of the ingredients. Serve.

Cheese the Old-Fashioned Way

The head salter does not weigh the salt; she scoops it up and sprinkles it with a twist of her hand. The gesture is magnificent in its sureness and unawareness, as though she were a divinity of the underground, fulfilling her function so that the earth may go on turning, but herself a hundred leagues above this fateful and monotonous round.

—Henri Pourrat, *The Roquefort Adventure*

THE BEST GNOCCHI I HAVE EVER EATEN were made from Bellwether Farms' sheep's-milk ricotta at Zuni Cafe in San Francisco. They were plump puffs, served with fresh, sautéed morel mushrooms and drizzled with butter. They were so light I could have eaten a few dozen.

I first tasted Bellwether Farms' cheese when the Ferry Plaza Farmers' Market began. Cindy Callahan sold her sheep's-milk cheeses from her spot right next to my bakery's stall. We often bought her Pepato cheese, studded with whole peppercorns, for our lunches. We cut it thinly, draped it on slices of our bread, and, if tomatoes were in season, topped the cheese with their dripping sweetness, then devoured these delicacies. The sharp edge of the cheese and the piquant pepper offset the sweetness of the tomato. In those early days of Bellwether Farms, Cindy only made sheep's-milk cheese a few times a week. She also sold pieces of lamb then, including bone-in stew meat, which I often took home for dinner and cooked slowly with sweet carrots and just-dug potatoes also purchased at the market.

During the years when I sold baked goods at the market, she encouraged me to visit her farm to see the cheese being made. One day, I took her up on her offer. I drove from San Francisco on a welcome clear day amid the torrents of rain in the El Niño winter. After parking near the farmhouse, I walked through a gate into a meadow with a fence on my left and headed up the hill, following her phone instructions of the previous day. Black-and-white cows with blue metal tags like fancy earrings grazed on the other side, stopping to look at me as I walked past. Far to the right were sheep and a few lambs. The climb got steeper as I walked through the ankle-high grass. The view back down the meadow was of lush rolling hills, verdant from the rain. At the top of the meadow stood a wooden barn with a tin roof. I heard voices at the far end of the building, found the door, and let myself in.

Cindy interrupted her work packaging cheese to show me around. Inside the cheese room, a vat held a hundred gallons of sheep's milk, slowly curdling from the addition of a bacteria starter and rennet. Cindy's son Liam would soon arrive to complete the process of making the milk into cheese. That day the vat of sheep's milk would become St. Andreas, named for the fault line that runs under the property. Other days, milk from a neighbor's Jersey cows is made into cheese. One of these cheeses, Carmody, is an aged wheel, golden from the high butterfat content of the Jerseys' milk. It has the smoothness of butter and a clean, fresh taste.

As we reminisced about the market, Liam and his wife, Diana, arrived. Liam explained how the milk had gotten to its present state—first it was pasteurized, then transferred to a stainless steel vat next to the pasteurizer. A special bacteria starter then changed the lactose in the milk into lactic acid, heightening the acidity and allowing the next step to occur. Vegetable rennet stirred into the vat coagulated the casein, the protein in the milk.

These are the same basic steps that produce all cheese, just as all bread is made from a fermented dough that contains flour, water, a leavening agent, and salt. And just as time, heat, handling, and age can vary the outcome of bread loaves, so do they affect the texture and flavor of cheese.

I started wondering about my attire as I saw Liam and Diana don knee-high rubber boots and ankle-length rubber aprons over their T-shirts and lightweight pants. Whatever happened next, there was going to be a lot of water involved. I was glad I was wearing old shoes with rubber soles. And I was already feeling too warm in a sweater and heavy jeans.

Diana showed me the development of the curd by pushing her index and middle finger into the quivering mass, then drawing her thumb through it to meet her fingers. It parted the way a thickening sauce parts in a pan when a spoon is drawn through it, but the consistency was different, more like soft Jell-O with small air pockets. Liam repeated the finger test. "It's time," he said.

They got out a square steel frame strung with taut wires that looked like an exotic musical instrument and attached handles to the vertical sides. Then they plunged it into one end of the vat and dragged it to the far side. Next they dragged it several times through the width. The wires cut the coagulated mass into curds, releasing the liquid whey. Then Liam and Diana leaned over the vat and churned with their arms. Now the mass was starting to turn into cheese. When the curds became firm enough, a bucket brigade started—Liam scooped a container of curds and whey and handed it to Diana, who poured it into waiting plastic molds riddled with small holes that rested on a table with a drain at one end. The next bucket went to Cindy. The whey gushed though the holes of the molds onto the table, some splashing on the floor, the rest whirling through the drain into plastic containers. Speed was important because the protein was starting to clot again. When all the curds were in the molds, Liam and Diana picked up each mold in both hands, and then, with a sharp flick of their wrists, dislodged each coagulating mass so that it flipped into the air, turned over, and landed upside down back in the mold.

The developing cheeses were flipped every fifteen minutes for two hours. As the curds lose liquid, they sink into the molds. The following day the cheese is salted and transferred to the aging room, where it will stay for two months.

The Callahans use the whey to make ricotta. It is an economically prudent way to use a by-product of cheese making, and it produces a highly sought-after cheese that enables restaurants to make things like the glorious gnocchi I ate at Zuni.

I left Liam and Diana and walked back to the farmhouse. Cindy was on the phone, in the middle of a complicated discussion about ewes, rams, veterinary visits, inoculations, and breeding. As I overheard her conversation, the complexity of the enterprise struck me. Making and aging highly respected cheese, taking orders, marketing, and trucking to farmers' markets was only half of it. Buying and breeding animals, providing pasture and supplemental feed, selling lambs, and milking ewes twice a day was the other half. Bellwether Farms is the first sheep dairy in California—started by a family with no experience in animal husbandry or cheese making.

Cindy finished her call and hung up. Running her hand through her short-cropped hair, she declared, "I'm getting too old for this!" Then, her mouth relaxing into a smile and her blue eyes twinkling, she said, "But I love it."

Although Mary Keehn has been making goat cheese at Cypress Grove Chevre in McKinleyville, California, since 1984, I didn't notice any of her cheeses until just recently. As I was looking over a sumptuous cheese selection at the tony Oakville Grocery in Healdsburg, a small, 3½-inch round, cut in half, caught my eye. Dark ash covered it and ran in a thin line through the center, like Morbier, but this cheese was stark white. It was Humboldt Fog, named for the weather on the Northern California coast. I asked for a taste. It was dry and creamy at the same time, rich and piquant, with the distinctive aroma of goat. I loved it, bought a large piece, and knew I had to visit her.

"What size shoes do you wear?" Mary asked at the end of our phone conversation. "Nine," I answered. "Then my daughter's boots will probably fit you," she said. I had planned on wearing the same shoes that got me through the visit to Bellwether, but this time it looked as though I would graduate to boots. There was also another graduation in store for me.

There wasn't any fog in Humboldt County the day I drove to Cypress Grove. Cresting the hill just north of Arcata, Clam Beach was a half-moon of sand lapped by shimmering blue water reflecting the sunlight. A few turns on narrow winding roads led me to the address. I walked into the office. Mary's oldest daughter and partner in the business greeted me. She fetched Mary from the "plant."

Mary entered, wearing knee-high white boots, sweat pants, and a white jacket, her long brown hair secured in a hair net. I donned boots and a jacket and we went into a small packing room. Mary was in a hurry. Cheeses needed labels for an order. When that task was finished, she handed me a hairnet and we stepped into the production room. Workers had started the cheese-making process the previous day. Now the milk sat in big plastic tubs. Two men worked at slanted tables covered with small perforated plastic molds, ladling the set curds from the tubs into the molds, where they will become Cypress Grove Chevre. The whey from seven tables dripped, dripped into containers, sounding like a soothing waterfall. "We start with six hundred gallons of milk and an eight-ounce ladle," Mary said. Although the work is extraordinarily laborious, it is the only way to get the special texture of this cheese, which is moist and silky yet holds its shape. (Campton Place Restaurant in San Francisco serves three scoops of this cheese on a plate with a potato truffle *gálette*—a trompe l'oeil twist on pie à la mode.) The workers fill the molds, leave them to drain, then fill and drain them a second time before turning them out of the molds and salting them. Then a worker turns each four-ounce cheese by hand each day during the short aging time. There are hundreds of them. "People wonder why the cheese is expensive; I wonder why it doesn't cost more," exclaimed Mary.

"Do you want to ladle some?" asked Mary. Here was my chance: my graduation from an observer to a participant. I was about to become a cheese maker. "Feel this," she said as she pressed her outstretched fingers on the top of a tub of set curds. I felt it with the flat of my hand, then pushed a finger into the gelatinous mass, remembering my visit to Bellwether. Mary recoiled slightly but said nothing. In the back of my brain, I knew that it was something I shouldn't have done. Mary demonstrated ladling the cheese. "The objective is to break the curds as little as possible." "You should have yelled at me when I poked it," I said. She only smiled. The task seemed simple enough for an eight-year-old. We worked side by side. After I had scooped a layer, I glanced into Mary's tub. It looked like a beach with carefully placed indentations, as if someone had pressed a ball into the sand in neat rows—the breaks in the curd clean, the edges touching, each depression half full of whey. My tub looked like a hailstorm had pounded the same tranquil beach—pockmarked, small pieces of curd swimming in a pool of whey. "When you have small curds mixed with whey like that, you can scoop them into this bucket before you begin ladling another row," Mary said diplomatically. After scooping, I poured the contents of the bucket into cheesecloth-draped baskets. When they're full, a worker ties them at the top, then hangs the big balls from a steel rod, their dripping whey adding to the waterfall sounds in the room. This curd is molded into different shapes, many of which are then aged.

We left our tubs for the men to finish and went into the molding room, where I saw round after round of Humboldt Fog. The room was humid and cold, the resting cheeses enveloping us in a mouthwatering aroma. When Mary first started making these aged cheeses, no one would buy them. Californians were just getting used to fresh goat cheese then, timidly crumbling it onto salads and spreading it on toasted slices of baguette. Now people are more accepting, and with the return of the cheese platter, aged goat cheese may hit its stride.

The return of the cheese platter signals the rejuvenation of a taste for good cheese. I remember the opening of a cheese store on 24th Street in San Francisco in the early 1970s. People bought pounds of triple cream cheese, the higher the fat content the better. Then cheese became a bad word. People worried about cholesterol and saturated fat, and cheese sales plummeted. Slowly, people are being coaxed back to eating small quantities of cheese. Traci Des Jardins' restaurant, Jardinière, has a temperature-controlled room for its cheese selection. Wine bars offer cheese. Three years ago Daphne Zepos was appointed cheese buyer at the Campton Place Hotel. She traveled to Europe, visiting out-of-the-way farms where cheese was made. Now she carefully chooses cheeses for a trolley that she rolls through the restaurant. Sidney and I sometimes go to the bar adjacent to the restaurant to sip martinis. On a recent visit, the cheese trolley was prominently displayed, holding a luscious selection. Daphne appeared and circulated among the bar tables, suggesting a small plate of cheese to those drinking wine. More than one table accepted. She's waiting for a great Gorgonzola to arrive. Then she plans to offer a "Blue Plate" in the bar—three blue cheeses paired with wines, perhaps a Sauternes, a light port, and a Beaumes-de-Venise. The sales are slowly climbing.

An ancient food that humbly began as a way to preserve milk is back in the spotlight—selected after careful auditions, pampered in temperature-controlled chambers, elegantly displayed, and elevated to separate billing as an important part of a meal.

Ricotta Gnocchi

The sublime gnocchi made from Bellwether Farms' sheep's-milk ricotta that I ate at Zuni Cafe made me call Judy Rodgers to find out how she made them. Then, a hunk of Bellwether cheese in hand, I headed for my kitchen.

The amount of flour needed in the gnocchi may not always be the same. Make the recipe and cook one. If it falls apart during or after cooking, add another teaspoon of flour to the cheese mix.

Knowing that not everyone can get Bellwether cheese, I tried these with different brands of ricotta. The type that is available in grocery store dairy cases does not work. It lacks the structure necessary to hold the gnocchi together. However, there is a good mail-order source for ricotta: the Mozzarella Company, 2944 Elm Street, Dallas, TX 75226, 800-798-2954. I used their cow's-milk ricotta as well as the half cow/half goat ricotta. Both were delicious and worked well in this recipe, although the cheese with the goat's milk was wetter.

The mixture needs to chill for an hour in the refrigerator before poaching.

4 SERVINGS, ABOUT 32 PIECES

The gnocchi

> 1 pound ricotta cheese
> 1 ounce (about ⅔ cup) grated imported Parmesan or dry Jack cheese
> 2 extra-large eggs
> 1 tablespoon unsalted butter, melted
> 2 teaspoons unbleached all-purpose flour, plus 1 cup for shaping gnocchi

The sauce

> 4 tablespoons (2 ounces) unsalted butter
> 1 tablespoon chopped fresh sage, about 4 large leaves

Make the gnocchi mix

Put the ricotta, Parmesan, eggs, butter, and flour in a medium bowl and mix vigorously with a wooden spoon until everything is well combined. Cover the bowl with plastic wrap and refrigerate for 1 hour.

Cook the gnocchi and make the sauce

Fill a large skillet with water and add 2 teaspoons salt. Bring to a slow simmer. Place a cup of flour on a piece of waxed paper or in a shallow dish. Shape the gnocchi by scooping up a generous teaspoon of the cheese mix, transferring it to a second teaspoon, then sliding it onto the flour. Roll the football shapes around gently in the flour. Poach a test gnocco for 6 minutes to see if the mixture contains enough flour, adding more to the remaining mix if the gnocco falls apart. Shape a fourth of the mixture, roll them in flour, and put them into the barely simmering water. Cook for 6 minutes. They will float to the surface as they cook. Transfer them with a large slotted spoon or a skimmer to heated bowls and keep them warm. Shape and poach the rest.

While the gnocchi are poaching, melt the butter in a small saucepan. When it is bubbling, add the sage and turn off the heat.

When all the gnocchi are cooked, moisten them with the sage butter and serve. Pass salt and pepper separately.

SPRING LAMB STEW

I sometimes bought lamb stew meat from Cindy Callahan of Bellwether Farms during the early days of the Ferry Plaza Farmers' Market, when she sold both lamb meat and sheep's-milk cheese. The meat from the young lamb was tender and flavorful. Choose meat from young animals if you can get it.

The meat gets browned in the oven with vegetables, whose caramelized exteriors give flavor to the stew. The bones also add to the flavor, as well as to the consistency. Add a parsnip for a different twist. If the carrots are very tender, there's no need to peel them. This stew can be made a few days ahead and reheated.

4 SERVINGS

The meat

*2½ pounds young lamb shoulder meat with bones, cut into
  2-inch cubes
2 small carrots, cut in 1-inch pieces
2 stalks celery, cut in 1-inch pieces
½ onion, coarsely chopped*

The stew

*3 tablespoons olive oil
2 young leeks, thinly sliced
1 tablespoon all-purpose flour
1 cup (8 ounces) dry white wine
2 cups (16 ounces) water
Seasonings: 1 bay leaf, ½ teaspoon herbes de Provence,
  ½ teaspoon salt
¼ teaspoon pepper
2 carrots, peeled and sliced ¼ inch thick
2 stalks celery, peeled and sliced ¼ inch thick
1 small parsnip, peeled and sliced ¼ inch thick
1¼ pounds golf-ball-size potatoes*

Prepare the meat

Preheat the oven to 500°F.

Place the meat, carrots, celery, and onion in a single layer in a roasting pan. Put the pan in the oven and roast until the meat and vegetables are brown and bits are caramelizing on the pan, 15 to 20 minutes. Stir them a few times as they roast. Don't let them burn.

Prepare the stew

While the meat is roasting, heat the olive oil in a medium flame-proof casserole. Add the leeks and cook until they start to soften but not brown, 5 minutes. Sprinkle the flour over the leeks and cook until the flour absorbs the oil, another few minutes. Set the casserole aside.

When the meat is brown, transfer it with tongs to the casserole. Pour the wine into the roasting pan. Bring it to a boil, scraping the browned bits from the pan. Strain the liquid into the casserole, pressing down on the vegetables. Bring the liquid to a simmer, stirring to cook the flour. Add the water and seasonings. Cover and cook at a low simmer for 1 hour.

Add the carrots, celery, parsnip, and potatoes and enough additional water to almost cover them. Bring the liquid back to a simmer and cook until the vegetables are soft and the meat is tender and separating from the bones, about 45 minutes.

Serve the stew warm in soup bowls with crusty bread.

CHEESE CUSTARD TARTLETS

Commercial ricotta purchased in the grocery store is transformed into an airy custard that puffs to a brown dome on a dough base in these tartlets. They are equally good at breakfast or for a dinner dessert. Orange blossom water, found in Middle Eastern stores, gives them a unique taste. If you can't find the water, substitute the finely chopped zest (but not the white pith) of 1 orange. Use tartlet pans with removable bottoms.

6 TARTLETS

The tart dough

12 tablespoons (6 ounces) unsalted butter at room temperature
½ cup (3½ ounces) granulated sugar
1 extra-large egg
½ teaspoon vanilla extract
1¾ cups (8½ ounces) unbleached all-purpose flour

The custard

1 cup (8 ounces) ricotta cheese
½ cup (3½ ounces) granulated sugar
6 extra-large egg yolks
¼ cup (1¼ ounces) unbleached all-purpose flour
Pinch salt
1 teaspoon orange blossom water
6 extra-large egg whites
2 tablespoons (1 ounce) granulated sugar

Make the tart dough

Put the butter in the bowl of a heavy-duty mixer. Beat it with the paddle until it is creamy. Add the sugar and beat until light and fluffy. In a separate bowl, beat the egg and vanilla together with a fork. With the mixer running, add the egg. Scrape the bowl and mix well. Add the flour all at once and mix at low speed until it is just incorporated. Remove the dough from the bowl, flatten it to a disk ½ inch thick on a piece of plastic wrap, cover it with more plastic wrap, and refrigerate for 1 hour, or up to 3 days. The dough can also be frozen, tightly wrapped, for 1 month.

Assemble and bake the tartlets

Preheat the oven to 400°F.

Have 6 tartlet pans ready, each 4¾ inches in diameter, with removable bottoms. Remove the dough from the refrigerator and roll it into a rectangle ⅛ inch thick on a lightly floured work surface. If the dough cracks and resists rolling, it is too cold. Let it warm a little, or pound it with a rolling pin, then proceed. Cut disks of dough a little larger than the tartlet pans. Line each pan with a round of dough, pressing it into the bottom edge. Chill them in the freezer while you make the custard.

Whisk the cheese, sugar, egg yolks, flour, salt, and orange blossom water together in a medium bowl. In another bowl, or in the bowl of a heavy-duty mixer, whisk the egg whites with 1 tablespoon of the sugar until they are frothy and opaque. Add the remaining tablespoon of sugar and beat the whites until soft peaks form. They will still look wet. Fold a third of the whites into the cheese mixture, then fold in the rest. Distribute the custard among the tart pans. Put the pans on the middle shelf of the oven and bake until the tops are browned and domed and the pastry is brown, 25 to 30 minutes. Serve slightly warm.

Sweetened Goat Cheese
with Strawberries

This is a modification of the French dessert *coeur à la crème*, sweetened *fromage blanc* drained in a special heart-shaped mold. Using goat cheese gives it a special taste. I prefer Cypress Grove Chevre, but if that isn't available use a fresh goat cheese that isn't too dry. If *fraises des bois*, the tiny perfumed strawberries, are available, serve them whole with the cheese and make the purée out of regular strawberries.

Make this the day before you plan to serve it.

4 SERVINGS

    4 ounces fresh goat cheese
    2 tablespoons powdered sugar, sifted
    1 teaspoon vanilla extract, preferably Madagascar Bourbon
    ¾ cup (6 ounces) heavy whipping cream
    2 pints ripe strawberries
    Granulated sugar to taste

Whisk the cheese, powdered sugar, vanilla, and ¼ cup of the cream together. Whip the remaining ½ cup cream until soft peaks form, and fold it into the cheese. Line a small sieve with three layers of cheesecloth and spoon in the cheese, flattening the top. Set the sieve over a bowl and refrigerate overnight.

The next day, wash and hull the berries. Purée one pint of the berries in a food processor. Add sugar to taste and heat in a saucepan until the sugar is melted; don't cook the berries.

Just before serving, turn the molded cheese onto a serving plate. Remove the cheesecloth. Slice the remaining berries and arrange them around the cheese. Serve each person a large spoonful of cheese, some berries, and a generous spoonful of purée.

Oysters in Time

Growing up in Pittsburgh, Pennsylvania, I didn't eat much fresh fish. This was before the days when live crustaceans and just-picked produce were jetted around the country. Occasionally when we were "downtown," my mother would stop at a fish store that had whole fish displayed on beds of ice. The store had an open wall that faced the street, with awnings to deflect the sun. At the end of the day, the wooden floor was slippery from the dripping ice. This is the only fish market that I remember from my childhood. After making a selection, we would leave with our purchase in a special bag containing dry ice that would cool the fish during the streetcar ride home.

Once, my mother bought a jar of oysters at that market, uncooked, slithery things suspended in liquid. I was very suspicious. Floured and fried, those were the first oysters I ever ate. Because they tasted so radically different from anything in my food repertoire, my initial reaction was cautious. Probably the only reason I tried them at all was because my parents were eating them with gusto. This oyster dinner was repeated on the occasional Friday night, and in time I came to like them. (It would be many years later, on the coast of Brittany, that I would learn to love raw oysters.)

Perhaps due to the family's acceptance of the oysters, or because of a nostalgia for his own childhood, my father announced one Christmas Eve that we were having oyster stew for dinner. Evidently, this was *the* thing to have for that celebratory meal when he was growing up, much as it is de rigueur for the French to begin a Christmas *réveillon* with oysters on the half shell today.

There was only one problem: he didn't have the recipe. This led to a search for my grandmother's old cookbook, the one with the broken bindings and children's scribblings on the pages. At last it was unearthed and the recipe found. It was the simplest of dishes—the oyster liquid was first heated and then combined with hot milk. The oysters were poached in this mixture just until the edges shriveled and then the stew was poured into hot bowls and sprinkled with oyster crackers.

This new experience had the same taste as the now-familiar fried oysters, but the texture was something else. Nonetheless, I slurped it down, popping an extra cracker into my mouth with each bite of oyster for the crunch that was missing.

My parents were celebrating this dish with much fanfare, and their mood quickly transferred to me. I think it was more the conviviality of the moment than the taste of the dish, but I will always fondly associate oyster stew with Christmas Eve.

Today, in San Francisco, those same rounded streetcars that carried us home have recently been resurrected from cities all over the country, given new paint jobs, and installed on Market Street. And I still occasionally buy shucked oysters in jars. They are from the Johnson's Oyster Company, a family-owned business in Inverness, north of San Francisco. The oysters that they farm, *Crassostrea gigas,* were transplanted from Japan to the Pacific Northwest in 1902. Charles W. Johnson, originally a wheat farmer in Oklahoma, moved to Washington and switched to fishing in 1939. Oysters caught his attention, and he made several trips to Japan, where he learned to cultivate oysters on long wires stuck in the mud. In 1957 he bought 1,000 acres on Schooner Bay, an inlet of Drake's Estero, and started cultivating oysters. The enterprise grew and, by the time of his death in 1992, was selling more than 7 million oysters a year. Many of the family members carry on the business.

One of them, who has been in the business "all of my life," sells jars of shucked oysters, as well as oysters in the shell, at farmers' markets. When I asked him if I could visit the operation, he encouraged me to "just show up some afternoon. Someone will show you around."

I headed north on an October afternoon. The sun was shining and the air was warm, but I threw a sweater in the car, not knowing whether the coast would be blanketed in fog. The weather held, and as I turned onto the road leading to Johnson's Oyster Company, it was easy to tell what business they are in. The gravel road wasn't gravel at all, but crushed oyster shells.

The afternoon that I arrived two men were hunched over disassembled pieces of a large machine, clearly not in the mood to show someone around. So I explored on my own. Three men were dumping oysters from blue milk crates onto a conveyor, where they separated and washed them. Animated activity was going on behind closed doors marked "Employees only. No Admittance." I obeyed the sign. There were other signs. A huge one taking up the side of a building explained in detail that dogs must stay in cars, another on the side of a large trash container admonished, "Take your trash with you," and a third sternly stated, "We can't open oysters. Don't ask." I didn't dare. Perhaps these pronouncements were vestiges of the days of Charles Johnson, who had the reputation of being somewhat of a character, with strong opinions ranging from philosophy to politics.

I found a small retail section and was helped by a man who is Johnson's grandson, also in the business all his life. He had a weathered look that made it hard to tell his age. A couple arrived and bought fifty oysters in the shell. "I hope you brought ice, 'cause our ice machine is broken," stated the grandson. I chose a jar of shucked oysters, size small. When I asked how long they would keep, I was told ten days. "You have to refrigerate them, though. Just don't throw them in the back seat of your car for a week. I have to tell people this. You won't believe what they will do," he said, rolling his eyes, as if he had been asked the same questions a million times.

On Tomales Bay, a different style of oyster farming has been going on since 1982. At the Hog Island Oyster Company, a group of men wearing rubber aprons and tall boots were cleaning oysters on a large outdoor table. Next to them stood large tanks filled with salt water holding those already cleaned. John Finger, who owns the company with fellow marine biologists Terry Sawyer and Michael Watchorn, interrupted his work for a few minutes to talk to me. Knee-high boots protected the legs of his jeans. A long-sleeved shirt, wide-brimmed hat, and dark glasses shielded him from the October sun. In addition to the *Crassostrea gigas*, which they call Hog Island Sweetwater, they also farm the flat Belon oyster, *Ostrea edulis*; and Kumamotos, *Crassostrea sikamea*. Finger grew up on the East Coast, eating clams and fish but not oysters. An interest in aquaculture brought him to California, where he expected to stay five years. His first job with a large producer in Morro Bay led to an opportunity to start oyster farming in the tiny village of Marshall on Tomales Bay.

Raising more than one type of oyster appealed to Finger because he can offer different types at different times of the year. Another advantage is that different diseases strike different varieties; the parasite that damages the Belons both here and in France doesn't attack the others. Most of the oysters go to restaurants, although 25 percent of the sales are to people willing to drive to Tomales Bay for excellent fresh oysters in the shell.

Like most other oyster farmers, he buys spat, the oyster larvae, from a nursery. The larvae attach themselves to finely chopped pieces of shell. They are so small that several thousand fit into a screen cylinder about a yard long. Many cylinders are filled and then suspended in the water, where they are tumbled occasionally to help the oysters grow uniformly. In time, the oysters are transferred to large wire cages set on plastic pipes above the bay floor. The mature oysters are harvested after about nine months. This method, perfected in the 1960s, differs from the much older one used by the Johnsons. Some people think these oysters are leaner and superior in taste.

Fifteen years after arriving in California, Finger is still farming oysters and plans to buy the additional equipment needed to grow even more. He has changed from not even eating oysters to depending on them for his livelihood.

I'm glad that both these businesses exist—the old way and the new. We pan-fried the Johnson oysters and ate the Hog Island Sweetwaters on the half shell. It would be nostalgic to have oyster stew this Christmas Eve. Now I know I'm dreaming. My children would never eat it.

OYSTER STEW

This is an adaptation of the recipe from my Irish grandmother's tattered cookbook.

4 SERVINGS

> 3 tablespoons (1½ ounces) butter
> 3 tablespoons chopped onion
> 3 tablespoons chopped leafy celery tops
> 2 jars (10 ounces each) shucked oysters, size small
> 2½ cups (20 ounces) whole milk
> Salt and pepper
> Croutons: 4 slices rye bread (recipe follows), cut into cubes and
>   toasted

Warm 4 serving bowls.

Melt the butter in a large saucepan. Add the onion and cook over medium heat until it is soft and limp but not brown. Add the celery tops for the last few minutes.

Drain the oysters, saving the liquid.

Add the milk to the saucepan. Heat until very warm, but just below a simmer. Add the reserved oyster liquid, oysters, salt, and pepper. Cook without boiling, stirring gently, until the edges of the oysters shrivel and they become firmer, 1 to 2 minutes. If the oysters are very small, such as Olympias, the cooking time will be less. Don't let the liquid boil, or it may curdle.

Ladle the stew immediately into the warm bowls, sprinkle with croutons, and serve. A tossed green salad or a salad of sliced apples and Belgian endive is a good accompaniment.

PAN-FRIED OYSTERS
WITH QUICK TARTAR SAUCE

These oysters are served with an easy sauce made from ingredients that most people have on the shelves of their refrigerator door. The entire preparation takes about 20 minutes.

4 SERVINGS

The tartar sauce

> *1 cup commercial mayonnaise*
> *1 tablespoon capers*
> *1 tablespoon chopped cornichon pickle*
> *1 tablespoon finely chopped shallot*
> *2 tablespoons finely chopped parsley*
> *2 teaspoons cornichon pickle brine*
> *1 teaspoon caper brine*
> *½ teaspoon Worcestershire sauce*
> *Salt and pepper*

The oysters

> *⅔ cup (3⅓ ounces) all-purpose flour*
> *⅓ cup (1½ ounces) fine white cornmeal*
> *Salt and pepper*
> *½ cup safflower oil*
> *2 jars (10 ounces each) shucked oysters, drained*

Make the tartar sauce

Mix all of the ingredients thoroughly and spoon into a serving dish.

Cook the oysters

Heat 4 serving plates in an oven at 140°F.

Mix the flour, cornmeal, and salt and pepper in a large bowl. Heat the oil in a 10-inch skillet until it is almost smoking. Coat 4 of the oysters with the flour and cornmeal and put them in the skillet. Cook over medium-high heat until the oysters are browned, about 1 minute. Gently turn them and brown the other side. Transfer to a plate lined with paper towels and keep them warm in the oven while you cook the rest, 4 at a time.

Divide the cooked oysters among the serving plates. Serve at once, passing the tartar sauce on the side. Red cabbage coleslaw makes a colorful accompaniment.

RYE BREAD TO SERVE WITH OYSTERS

In Brittany, the origin of most of France's oysters, as well as in the brasseries of Paris, thin slices of rye bread are always served with oysters on the half shell. The plate of bread is tucked under a stand on which the shellfish rest on a bed of ice and seaweed. Restaurants in San Francisco, such as Zuni Cafe, replicate this practice. The assertive taste of the grain is a perfect counterpoint to the briny, sweet oysters.

This bread is made with a sponge starter, which encourages the fermentation, so less yeast is used. This method also accentuates the taste of the rye. Although it adds to the overall time, mixing the sponge takes only few minutes.

2 LOAVES

The sponge
> 1 cup cold tap water
> 2 teaspoons active dry yeast
> 1½ cups (7½ ounces) rye flour

The dough
> 1 cup minus 2 tablespoons (7 ounces) cold tap water
> 1 cup (5 ounces) rye flour
> 2 cups (10 ounces) unbleached bread flour
> 2½ teaspoons salt

Make the sponge

Pour the water into a medium-size mixing bowl. Sprinkle the yeast on top and let it dissolve and become creamy, about 5 minutes. Add the flour and mix with a wooden spoon. Cover the bowl with plastic wrap and leave at 75°F for 2 hours. The batter will rise and bubble slightly on the surface.

Mix the dough

Pour the water into the bowl of a heavy-duty mixer. Scrape in all of the sponge. Add the flours and salt and knead the dough with the hook for 8 minutes. The dough should form a soft ball on the hook. Add small amounts of water or flour as needed. Rye doughs are stickier than other doughs; don't add too much additional flour.

Cover the bowl with plastic wrap and let the dough rise at 75°F until almost doubled in bulk, about 2 hours.

Shape and bake the bread

Preheat the oven to 450°F for 45 minutes, with a baking stone on the middle shelf and a baking pan on the floor of the oven. Set the baking pan on a rack just above the heating element if the oven is electric.

Turn the dough onto a floured work surface and divide it into halves. Shape each half into a loaf. Lay a kitchen towel on a baking pan and flour it. Put the loaves on the towel, seam side up, about 5 inches apart. Make a pleat in the towel between the loaves to keep them from touching. Cover the loaves with another kitchen towel and slide the baking pan inside a large plastic bag. Let rise at 75°F until the loaves almost double in bulk, about 45 minutes.

When the dough is ready for the oven, bring 2 cups water to a boil.

Turn the loaves over, now seam side down, onto a well-floured baking peel or cookie sheet. Slash each loaf down the center with a single-edge razor blade. Slide the loaves onto the baking stone. Immediately pour the boiling water into the baking pan on the bottom of the oven and close the door. *Caution:* This will cause a burst of steam. Wear long oven mitts. Don't open the oven door for the first 10 minutes of baking. The bread is finished when it is well browned and sounds hollow when thumped on the bottom, about 30 minutes. Thoroughly cool the loaves on a rack before slicing them.

A Unique Market

IT WAS A NOVEMBER MORNING. I walked my usual route in Golden Gate Park—past the woman with the sword going through the motions of an ancient martial art, past the tai chi group flowing from one stance to another, past the seniors counting to their calisthenics, past the watchful eyes of the horses in their stalls, and around the long periphery of Speedway Meadow. Invigorated, I climbed into the car and headed to one of my favorite shopping places, the block of Irving Street between 22nd and 23rd Avenues. I found a lucky parking spot and walked a block to the produce store.

An abundance of fruit and vegetables spilled into outdoor bins crowding the sidewalk. Inside, a clientele speaking English, Greek, Cantonese, Russian, and what sounded like other Eastern European languages jostled its way over the sawdust-covered floor, hefting cabbages, picking over beans, and eyeing the prices, while the radio blared top tunes from the fifties. A restaurant owner bought cases of apples, a sack each of onions and potatoes, and enough parsley to feed a family for a year. My cart filled as if by magic; I always buy more than I intend. I left the store with a heavy sack in each hand, the top of a fennel bulb protruding from one, the other weighted down with persimmons.

I don't remember how I discovered this store; I think it was during the early years of the bakery. I often drove the delivery truck there in the afternoon, looking for bargains. Once, fifteen crates of strawberries didn't make it into the store; they went from the sidewalk where they were being unloaded into my truck instead. Back at the bakery, we paired them with rhubarb and made preserves.

One fall day years ago I saw a wooden box holding fifteen or twenty pounds of green olives. I had never seen uncured olives for sale. A sign discouraged would-be tasters—"Do not eat. Very bitter." An uncontrollable force overcame me and I bought the box. Sidney eyed it suspiciously when he saw it on our kitchen counter. "What are you going to do with those?" he asked. I had to admit that I didn't know exactly. He smiled and shook his head at my latest culinary undertaking. I called the University of California Extension Service and requested a pamphlet on curing olives. It contained several warnings set apart by bold black boxes—"If, for any reason, you suspect the edibility of olives, do not taste them." "Place the box outdoors so that the brine formed will not ruin the floor." "Do not taste any olives that develop a rancid or foul odor." The last page detailed antidotes for lye burns. "What have I gotten myself into?" I wondered. Most of the recipes called for a lye bath to leach out the olives' bitterness. I went to a grocery store and found a box of lye next to the Drano. Then I set up an olive-curing operation in the basement. The olives in the lye solution needed to be checked every twelve hours to determine whether the lye had reached the pits. (The color of the olives changes as the lye solution penetrates them.) This was during a time when I usually worked twelve hours a day at the bakery, so at 5:00 A.M. I made a detour on my way to work. I sloshed the olives in the lye solution, changing it if necessary, then repeated the inspection twelve hours later. After the lye treatment, the olives needed repeated rinsings in water to remove the taste. I then put them in jars with garlic cloves and small dried red chiles, filling the jars with a solution of vinegar and salt water. In a few weeks they had assimilated the flavors. Their taste was pleasant, but their texture was slightly mushy, lacking the crispness of good olives. I think I left them in the lye too long.

My next olive adventure was with ripe black ones that I bought at the store. I packed them in salt in small plastic tubs and kept them in the kitchen cupboard under the sink. It took a long time for them to lose their moisture and become wrinkled, but when they were ready they were intensely flavorful, although a little salty.

I could just have purchased ready-to-eat olives at the Twenty-Second and Irving Market. There, shelves are weighted down with an array of them—shriveled black ones in jars, other black ones surrounded by salty water in plastic pouches, green ones from Greece and Israel, and pimiento-stuffed ones from California. They sit next to an international selection of tinned foodstuffs that includes cornichons from Turkey, preserves from Lebanon, teas, canned fava beans, gallon tins of olive oil, and fruit juices from Belgium. One of the owners always has a feather duster tucked into his back pocket that he uses to dust off the jars—not that they need it; they aren't there long enough.

The shoppers swap cross-cultural recipes as they make their selections, scrutinizing each bean or zucchini as if separating real coins from counterfeit. An Italian woman recites recipes for fresh cranberry beans and dismisses fava beans with a wave of her arm because they are part of Roman cuisine and she is from Milano. A portly gentleman tells a cashier his recipe for dandelion greens—boiled, like spinach, then drained and mixed with lemon juice, olive oil, and garlic. When he finishes his recitation, he parts with the comment, "They're delicious, and they're good for the blood." An elderly woman with a babushka over her head and a collapsible shopping cart at her side asks me the difference between a Russet and a white potato. I suspect she made her choice by the price, not their cooking characteristics. A Sicilian woman intones the virtues of escarole—"Chop it and cook it with olive oil and garlic. Mix it with pasta. Or you can even eat it raw, like salad." An Asian woman assures me that if I eat brussels sprouts and cabbage I won't get cancer.

The store is always full, but the days right before holidays bring even larger crowds, sometimes impatient. "What, no broccoli?" cries an employee from the post office across the street, a stricken look on his face. "You'll have it tomorrow, won't you?" The storekeepers can barely keep the shelves full. They wheel hand trucks from the back piled high with cases of celery, carrots, cranberries, and squash. Chestnuts spill from burlap bags. Ten-pound sacks of rice—basmati, brown, and jasmine—are stacked eight feet high. The checkout lines clog the aisles, making it almost impossible to get to the mushrooms. On the radio, earnest voices croon "Three Coins in the Fountain," then "In the Chapel in the Moonlight."

Or, when it's closer to Christmas, "Blue Christmas" and "My Favorite Things."

The last time I bought raw olives there was about four years ago, just before Thanksgiving. The timing couldn't have been worse; Thanksgiving was an extraordinarily busy time at the bakery, and I really didn't have time for a nonbaking project. But they were small, and unblemished, and I couldn't resist. I waited in line, the bread rack pressing against my right shoulder, passing carts bumping my left leg, as I balanced the box of olives on top of my cart. The cashier, wearing a colorful smock decorated with fruit and vegetables, looked dazed. I finally got out of the store and loaded everything into the back of my truck. During the drive home, I came to terms with my irrational purchase. A friend had told me that he wanted to learn how to cure olives. I gave him the box, along with all the information I had on olives. He water-cured them, then added citrus and spices. It has become my favorite recipe.

FUSILLI WITH ESCAROLE

Tempted by the beautiful escarole a Sicilian woman was praising at the Twenty-Second and Irving Market, I bought a head and combined it with pasta for dinner. Other sturdy greens such as Swiss chard or giant red mustard could be used instead. Use your best olive oil to moisten the pasta when it is combined with the cooked greens.

This makes a simple dinner with crusty bread.

4 TO 6 SERVINGS

4 tablespoons (2 ounces) olive oil
3 cloves garlic, finely chopped
Large pinch dried red pepper flakes
1 head escarole (about ¾ pounds), washed, shaken dry, and
  roughly chopped
½ teaspoon salt
1 pound dried fusilli pasta, preferably Italian
Several grinds black pepper

Begin heating a 6-quart pot of generously salted water for the pasta.

Heat 2 tablespoons of the olive oil in a 12-inch skillet. Add the garlic and red pepper and cook for about a minute over medium heat, until the garlic just starts to brown. Add the escarole and salt, and cover the skillet. Cook over medium heat until the escarole is tender but still holds its shape, about 8 minutes.

When the water is boiling, add the pasta, give it a stir, and return it to the boil.

When the pasta is al dente, drain it and return it to the pot. Add the escarole, the remaining 2 tablespoons olive oil, and pepper to taste. Toss all together and serve immediately in heated bowls.

STRAWBERRY-RHUBARB PRESERVES

Use red-to-the-center berries and field-grown rhubarb. The rhubarb gives these preserves a wonderful texture that just isn't possible with strawberries alone. It also provides the acidity that the berries lack, so additional pectin isn't necessary.

The actual cooking takes place after 24 hours of macerating, so start a day before you want to make the preserves.

9 PINTS

> *6 pounds strawberries (buy 8 pint baskets so that the net weight after hulling will be correct)*
> *3 pounds rhubarb (buy 4 pounds)*
> *6 pounds granulated sugar (about 15 cups)*
> ***Canning tools:** a scale, pint jars with two-part lids, a large pot that will hold all the jars, a noncorroding 8-quart pot (or a copper canning kettle), a candy thermometer, a long-handled slotted spoon for skimming foam, a jar lifter, a ladle, and a widemouthed funnel*

Prepare the fruit

Wash and hull the berries. Cut them into quarters, or smaller if they are very large. Wash the rhubarb, trim the ends, and cut into ½-inch pieces. Toss both fruits together in a bowl. Choose another large bowl or a plastic container that fits into your refrigerator. Alternately layer the fruit with the sugar, beginning with fruit and ending with sugar. Cover and refrigerate for 24 hours, or up to 3 days.

Cook and process the preserves

Place a kitchen towel or a wire rack in the bottom of a large pot. Put 8 clean pint jars into the pot, cover with water, and bring to a boil. Boil for 20 minutes, then turn down the heat, leaving the jars in the hot water. Proceed with the recipe while the jars boil.

Pour the fruit into a large sieve or colander set into a heavy, non-corroding 8-quart pot. Use a copper canning kettle if you have one.

When the fruit has drained, set it aside. Scrape any undissolved sugar from the macerating container into the pot, and give the syrup a stir so that any undissolved sugar won't stick during the beginning stage of cooking. Using a candy thermometer, cook the sugar syrup over medium heat until it reaches 230°F (110°C), about 25 minutes, skimming the foam from the top. Add the drained fruit to the hot syrup and cook until the mixture is 217°F (103°C), another 25 minutes, skimming as necessary and stirring occasionally to distribute the heat evenly. The sound of the cooking will change from a quiet bubbling to a thick splatting when the preserves are the correct temperature.

During the last few minutes of cooking, turn up the heat under the jars and add clean lids to the boiling water. Remove a jar and a lid from the water (special jar-lifting tongs are available, but you can use regular metal tongs). Using a ladle, pour the preserves through a widemouthed funnel into the jar. Fill the jar to within ¼ inch of the top. Wipe the top of the jar and the rubber seal on the lid with a towel. Screw on the lid. Fill the rest of the jars. Return the filled jars to the pot of water. They should not touch each other, nor should they touch the bottom or sides of the pot. Add enough additional water to cover the jars by 1 inch. Bring the water to a boil, and boil for 20 minutes. Add 5 minutes for each 2,000 feet of elevation above sea level.

After processing, let the jars cool on a towel. When they are completely cool, check the seal on each one. The center of the lid will be depressed if the lid has sealed properly. If a jar did not seal, refrigerate it and consume the contents within a week. Store the sealed jars in a cool, dark place, where they will keep for at least a year.

These preserves are great in the Peanut Butter and Jelly Cake (page 18) from Citizen Cake.

WATER-CURED OLIVES

Olives straight from the tree contain bitter glucosides that make them inedible. Lye baths, salt packs, and soakings in water and brine solutions will remove the offending compound. I have used all of these techniques. My favorite is one based on a recipe in Maggie Klein's book, *The Feast of the Olive*, called "Anzonini's Water-Cured Green Olives." Green olives appear in some produce markets in November. If you can't find any, ask a local producer of olive oil to sell you some.

5 POUNDS OF SMALL OLIVES WILL PRODUCE ABOUT 8 PINTS

The olives

> *5 to 20 pounds unblemished green olives*
> *Lots of water*

The herbed vinegar/salt solution

> *Brine made from 5 tablespoons salt to 2 quarts water*
> *Peeled garlic cloves*
> *Lemon wedges*
> *Black peppercorns*
> *Cumin seeds or coriander seeds*
> *Sprigs of Greek oregano*
> *White wine vinegar (about 3 cups per 5 pounds of olives)*

Soak the olives

Slit each olive with a paring knife. Put them in a large plastic bucket and cover with cold water. Lay a few kitchen towels on top of the water to keep the olives immersed. Set the bucket in a cool place. Change the water every day. Start tasting the olives after 21 days. The olives will change color from green to a light brown. If they taste somewhat bitter, but faintly like olives, proceed to the next step. If they taste very bitter, continue soaking, changing the water every day for another week. The olives won't completely lose their bitterness; the vinegar and salt solution will cure them further.

Cure the olives

Heat the water and salt until the salt dissolves. Cool to room temperature. Wash pint jars, about 8 for every 5 pounds of olives. Into each jar put 1 clove of garlic, a lemon wedge, 2 black peppercorns, ⅛ teaspoon cumin seeds or coriander seeds, and a small sprig of oregano. Fill each jar with olives to ½ inch from the top. Pour white wine vinegar into the jars, filling them half full. Top off each jar with the brine solution. Screw on the lids. Do not process these olives in a water bath; they simply marinate in the vinegar-and-brine solution. Store in a cool, dark place or in the refrigerator for at least 2 weeks to let the flavors blend before serving. They will keep for at least 2 months, although I have kept them longer.

Microbakers

Bread in the Bay Area has come full circle since I opened my bakery in 1984. Then, only two types of bread were widely available. The long-established San Francisco sourdough bakeries made chewy white loaves with a tang in the taste. The other bread was sliced loaves, sealed in transparent wrapping, baked by a variety of companies and distributed to grocery stores. The European notion of baking and selling in the same location was just starting to appear. The bread that came out of these new artisanal bakeries was different—made without preservatives, sometimes baked on stones, European in look and taste.

People were becoming attuned to good bread and were growing more sophisticated. Every dining review in the *San Francisco Chronicle* included the restaurant's bread source. When I started selling handcrafted loaves baked on the premises, they were an instant success. I was a self-taught bread baker and had not really planned to make bread, but a friend wanted some for his food store, so we obliged. I found the recipes in books aimed at home bakers. Some we used just as they were; others I modified. Most of the early loaves were leavened with commercial yeast. Then I found a recipe for sourdough in a French baking book I had purchased on a trip to Paris. It involved soaking raisins in water until they fermented, then using the water to make a starter. It wasn't quite that simple—the initial fermentation took five days, then the starter had to be gradually strengthened by additions of more flour and water before a final dough was ready. Undaunted, we tackled the recipe and started making sourdough bread. The dough became our *pain au levain*, a football-shaped one-pound loaf that was dense, chewy, and distinctively sour. That same starter leavened a bread with sautéed onions. Eventually we added breads made with other starters, liquid batters that rested in buckets in the refrigerator. The demand snowballed. We couldn't make enough. The upper limit was dictated by the size of the bakery, and I didn't want to move to an ugly building in a dreary part of town just so we could make more bread. During our busiest times, we rarely exceeded a thousand loaves a night.

The new artisanal bakeries expanded, and it seemed like a new one opened every year. They started small but quickly became big. Daily production expanded from a few hundred loaves to tens of thousands. They moved to large plants. Bakers negotiated for supermarket shelf space and wrestled with buy-back policies. Trucks delivered bread south to the middle of the peninsula and north to the Napa Valley. The per capita bread consumption probably exceeded that of France. And the surge isn't over. Bakeries continue to open, fanning into the countryside, producing more and more, using increasingly sophisticated equipment.

In these huge bakeries, I fear that the notion of the artisan baker has been lost. Although the dough may still be touched by human hands, is it a caress, or just a fleeting gesture? Does the bread suffer?

There are a growing number of bakers who want to go back to simpler ways—shaping the dough, and sometimes even kneading it, by hand; keeping production small; working close to where they live. They struggle not with how much more bread they can make, but with how they can keep their work manageable and the quality high. They prefer the ovens of yesteryear—built of brick and heated with a roaring fire that penetrates every atom of stone, so that when the coals are swept out enough heat remains to bake two or three hundred loaves of bread. The artisans are making a comeback.

A soft-spoken man with an Australian accent and strong convictions, who designs wood-burning ovens, is seminal to this resurgence. He arrived at this distinction by a circuitous route. Fifteen years ago, Alan Scott was a blacksmith living on a boat in Tomales Bay, north of San Francisco. He had friends at the nearby Blue Mountain Center of Meditation who enlisted his help in building an oven. He didn't know much about ovens but worked with an architect to draw up plans. A mason did the brick-work; Alan forged the doors. It was a complicated affair, with dampers and various doors, built into an existing fireplace. Laurel Robertson of the Center subsequently wrote a book, *The Laurel's Kitchen Bread Book,* that included a recipe for bread fashioned from a Flemish whole wheat sour-dough. The day I visited Alan, he dragged an old, worn copy from a kitchen shelf. The end cover is a woodcut depicting Alan loading bread into an outdoor oven with his boat on the Bay in the background.

Alan was so impressed by the bread his friends were making that he decided he needed an oven so he could make his own. He researched oven-building techniques and, after a few prototypes, settled on the brick-lined model that he builds today. Then he started baking bread to support himself, using the same sourdough recipe as his friends. Twice a week, he fired the oven, baking about two hundred loaves, then various casseroles, and always a pot of beans when the oven cooled. His life revolved around his baking, the delivery schedule providing social contact and an opportu-nity to make friends. He started the baking process by grinding organi-cally grown wheat and kneading the dough by hand. "I had a mixer for a few months but got rid of it. It interfered with the process too much; I just stood there and watched it. It only saved a few minutes," he told me. He took on apprentices, sometimes offering hitchhikers shelter, telling them, "I'll give you a place to stay, but there's one catch—you have to help me make bread."

His notion of an ideal bakery is a small, self-contained unit: a house where the baker lives, and a wood-fired oven in an adjacent building. The baker delivers the bread. Alan knows a baker who is selling his business and moving to a smaller building in the same town, where he'll build a brick oven and start over. Another baker is opting out of the heavy pro-duction schedule where he works, building a small oven, and going out on his own. Alan likes the idea of clusters of small bakeries in the same town, sharing knowledge—the antithesis of competitive business practice. "They can't get too big; smaller is more profitable," he told me.

Although there is an oven behind Alan's Victorian house, now he concentrates on building ovens rather than baking in them, and he has established a business called Ovencrafters. The ovens that he designs prove that newer isn't always better. Although more sophisticated than ancient stone baking chambers—with insulated fireboxes and digital temperature indicators—these brick-lined domes have the same advantages as their predecessors. The heat radiates from the bricks for hours, giving the loaves a dark, chewy crust. Baking in these ovens provides a strong connection to the past.

Alan's emphasis has shifted from baking to building, but his own oven isn't completely idle. A former apprentice still travels from San Francisco once a week to bake in it. Alan lives thirty minutes from Petaluma, out in the country among rolling hills dotted with grazing cattle. On the day of my planned visit he was late, delayed at an auto repair shop. He hurried into the house, balancing a bag of groceries with broccoli sticking out of the top, draped his coat over a chair, and removed his snap-brim cap, evidently a signature piece of clothing. He had just showed me Laurel Robertson's book when he remembered that his son was waiting in Petaluma for a ride home. We jumped into his car and jounced along the road into town. He told me how his oven making had evolved, and he expressed admiration for the old clay ovens in Quebec. "They're very sophisticated. Because of their shape—a low mouth and a higher dome— they don't need a vent," he said. I decided not to mention the very primitive adobe oven Sidney and I built ourselves at our country house. It not only has a vent, its shape isn't even close to pictures I've seen of the Quebec ovens.

We also talked about the organisms that contribute to the taste and texture of sourdough bread. He believes that they originate in the soil, then transfer to the wheat and, over time, build up in a bakery, where they contribute to the integrity of the dough. "The health departments don't understand," he said vehemently. "The organisms are everywhere in a bakery—on the tables, on the baskets, on the bakers. They have to be there. The bakers depend on them. There's nothing wrong with wooden floors or wooden mixing troughs. They're good for the bread."

It was dusk and a drizzle was falling when we returned to the house. His former apprentice, dressed in jeans and a warm plaid shirt, stood in front of the oven, slowly rotating pitas to expose all their sides to the fire. "Ah, the hectic life of a baker," Alan quipped. Then his thoughts turned to dinner. "How hot is it?" he asked. "675," was her answer. "Too hot for a quiche. Maybe a soufflé," he said, stroking his beard as he headed back to the house.

In the small town of Point Reyes Station, Chad Robertson and Elisabeth Prueitt of Bay Village Wood Fire Baking have built a business from Alan Scott's philosophy. They converted a potter's studio beside their house into a baking room, one wall dominated by the mouth of Ovencrafters' largest model, which can hold seventy-five loaves. When I arrived one recent morning at 7:45 A.M., the last batch of bread was in the oven. Rustic loaves, stacked on their sides, cooled on shelves made of two-by-fours supported by simple iron hooks running the length of one wall. *Pain de campagne* sported well-browned, thick crusts. Cut open, the color tapered to that of caramelized sugar where the crust met the crumb. The interior was shiny with irregular holes and was flecked with bran. The bread tasted of wheat, slightly sour, the browned exterior contributing flavor to the whole loaf. Baguettes were made from the same dough, but with a higher crust-to-crumb ratio. Other loaves had polenta interspersed throughout, tipping the flavor scale toward sweetness.

Chad, dressed in a tan shirt and pants, and with a French baker's cloth hat on his head, was folding long lengths of cloth used to hold the rising dough. A few feet away a small table held large brown paper bags. A mixer and a sink tucked into a corner were the other furnishings. Flour dusted the wide-planked wooden floor. Several peels, almost the width of the room, hung just under the ceiling. It was a compact two hundred square feet.

Both Chad and Elisabeth are graduates of the Culinary Institute of America in Hyde Park, New York. A passion for baking took them to France, where they concentrated on the intricacies of sourdough and the peculiarities of wood-fired ovens. The French bakers didn't bake just bread in their ovens; they used them for *croissants* and delicate pastries as well, a dream of Elisabeth's for the future. The day I was there, she tried an experimental batch of chocolate pastries baked in dark metal cups. Even though the oven was 600 degrees, they baked perfectly.

Their sojourn in France over, they made their way to California, hoping to eventually open a bakery. Their friendship with Alan enabled that process. They lived in his house and perfected recipes in his oven. In the year and a half since they started, they have built their business to 250, sometimes 350 loaves at a time, baking four days a week, selling to retail stores and in farmers' markets. Using a very hands-on approach, Chad kneaded all of the dough by hand at first, but it became too much. He ordered a mixer from Belgium. It has one side-mounted hook that picks up the dough and slaps it against the side of the bowl, very similar to the motion of hand kneading. As gentle as it was, it still overworked the dough. Chad fiddled with the kneading process until he found a solution. He's contemplating a few more pieces of equipment, but not without hesitation. He vacillated, but finally decided to order a retarder, a temperature-controlled box where the shaped loaves will rise, giving him some free time in the evening. He's also contemplating a propane torch instead of a wood fire, to maintain the oven's temperature on the days when he doesn't bake.

"Have you thought of getting someone to help you?" I asked. "Lots of people have been interested in becoming apprentices," he answered. "But we really don't have a system here like they do in France where people aren't paid money—they're housed and taken care of. I'd like to start an apprentice program here but have people pay to rotate among the bakeries."

This could be the upsurge of the next bread metamorphosis—bakers schooled in artisanal ways, opening their own microbakeries, keeping an ancient tradition alive.

SOURDOUGH PUMPERNICKEL RYE BREAD

No commercial yeast is used in this dough. Instead, the bread rises from a starter of pumpernickel rye meal and water. Initially, it takes 3 days to make the starter; then it can be refrigerated and kept alive indefinitely.

Refresh the starter at least once a week, by adding 4 ounces of pumpernickel meal and 1 cup of water, then recovering it and returning it to the refrigerator. Always do this the evening before you plan to bake bread.

You can find pumpernickel rye meal in some health food stores, or order it from Bob's Red Mill, 5209 SE International Way, Milwaukie, OR 97222, 503-654-3215, or from King Arthur Flour, P.O. Box 876, Norwich, VT 05055-0876, 800-827-6836.

This is a compact loaf, with the grain sweetened by molasses and accentuated by caraway seeds. It makes great sandwiches.

2 LOAVES

The starter

> 2¼ cups (12 ounces) pumpernickel rye meal, added in ¾-cup (4-ounce) increments
> 3 cups (24 ounces) cold tap water, added in 1-cup (8-ounce) increments

The dough

> 1¼ cups (10 ounces) cold tap water
> ⅞ cup (7 fluid ounces or 9 ounces by weight) pumpernickel starter
> 2 tablespoons vegetable oil
> 1¾ ounces (2 tablespoons plus 1 teaspoon) molasses
> 2 tablespoons caraway seeds
> 1¼ cups (6¾ ounces) pumpernickel rye meal
> 3¼ cups (1 pound) unbleached all-purpose flour
> 2½ teaspoons salt

Make the starter

Mix ¾ cup (4 ounces) of the pumpernickel rye meal and 1 cup (8 ounces) of the water together in a medium bowl. Cover with plastic wrap and leave at room temperature until the surface is bubbly, about 48 hours.

Mix in a second dose of pumpernickel rye meal (¾ cup or 4 ounces) and water (1 cup or 8 ounces). Cover again with plastic wrap and leave at room temperature for 12 to 18 additional hours.

Mix in a third dose of rye meal and water in the same proportions as the first two. Cover with plastic wrap and refrigerate overnight. Now the starter can be used to make bread.

Make the dough

Put the water in the bowl of a heavy-duty mixer. Scrape in 7 fluid ounces of the starter. (Store the remaining starter in the refrigerator; it will keep indefinitely as long as you refresh it as described above.) Add the oil, molasses, caraway seeds, pumpernickel rye meal, flour, and salt. Knead the dough on low speed with a dough hook until the ingredients come together. Increase the speed to medium and knead the dough for 10 minutes.

Cover the bowl with plastic wrap, and leave it at 75°F until it doubles in volume, about 4 hours.

Shape the dough

Turn the dough out onto a lightly floured work surface. Divide it into halves. Shape each half into a round. Line medium-size bowls or baskets with floured kitchen towels. Place the rounds into the bowls, rough side up, and fold the ends of the towels over the dough. Slip the bowls into a large plastic bag. Leave them at 75°F until they double in bulk, about 3 hours.

Bake the bread

Place a large, empty baking pan at the lowest level of the oven.

Preheat the oven to 450°F for 45 minutes with baking stones on the middle rack.

When the dough is ready for the oven, bring 2 cups water to a boil.

Remove the bowls from the plastic bag. Turn the rounds onto a floured peel. Score the top of each round with a single-edge razor blade. Transfer the rounds to the stones in the oven with a flick of the wrist. Immediately pour the boiling water into the empty pan in the bottom of the oven and close the door. *Caution:* This will cause an immediate burst of steam. Wear oven mitts and stand back. Don't open the door for the first 10 minutes, or the steam will escape.

Bake the loaves until they are well browned and sound hollow when thumped on the bottom, 30 to 35 minutes. Cool on a rack.

Polenta Bread

Bay Village Baking, a microbakery north of San Francisco, produces a bread with polenta mixed into the dough, using a sourdough starter to leaven their loaves. This is a simpler version of their bread. Instead of a sourdough starter, this dough begins with yeast, then bubbles for 3 hours to improve its flavor before the final dough is mixed. Although a little toasted wheat germ adds to its complexity, it can be omitted.

1 LARGE LOAF

The starter
> 1¼ teaspoons active dry yeast
> ½ cup (4 ounces) cold tap water
> Scant cup (4½ ounces) unbleached all-purpose flour

The dough
> 1 cup (8 ounces) cold tap water
> ⅔ cup (3½ ounces) polenta
> 2½ cups (12½ ounces) unbleached all-purpose flour
> 2 teaspoons salt
> 2 tablespoons wheat germ, lightly toasted

Make the starter

Sprinkle the yeast over the water in a medium bowl. Wait until it dissolves and becomes creamy, about 5 minutes, then add the flour. Mix the soft dough well with a rubber spatula. Cover the bowl with plastic and leave at room temperature (75°F) until it doubles and the entire surface is bubbly, about 3 hours.

Make the dough

Pour the water in the bowl of a heavy-duty mixer. Scrape in the starter, then add the polenta, flour, salt, and wheat germ. Mix with a dough hook on medium speed until everything is combined, then knead the dough for 10 minutes, adding very small amounts of flour if the dough doesn't form a ball on the hook. Cover the bowl with plastic and leave at room temperature until it doubles, about 2 hours.

Shape the dough

Turn the dough onto a floured surface, knead it a few times, then shape it into a ball. Line a medium-size bowl or basket with a floured kitchen towel. Put the round into the bowl, rough side up, and fold the ends of the towel over the dough. Slip the bowl into a large plastic bag and leave at room temperature until the dough is doubled in bulk and will hold a finger imprint, about 1½ hours.

Bake the bread

Place a large, empty baking pan at the lowest level of the oven.

Preheat the oven to 425°F for 45 minutes with a baking stone on the middle rack.

When the dough is ready, bring 2 cups water to a boil.

Take the bowl out of the plastic bag. Turn the round onto a floured peel. Score the top of the round with a single-edge razor blade, then slide it onto the baking stone. Immediately pour the boiling water into the empty pan in the bottom of the oven and close the door. *Caution*: This will cause an immediate burst of steam. Wear oven mitts and stand back. Don't open the door for the first 10 minutes, or the steam will escape.

Bake until the bread is well browned and sounds hollow when thumped on the bottom, 45 to 50 minutes. Cool on a rack.

COUNTRY WHOLE WHEAT BREAD

I like to begin a bread dough by making a starter. This method allows a slow fermentation that gives the final bread depth and character. Although it adds a little more time from start to finish, the actual mixing of the starter takes only a few minutes. For flour sources, see Sourdough Pumpernickel Rye Bread on page 211.

2 LOAVES

The starter
> 1¾ cups (14 ounces) cold tap water
> ½ teaspoon active dry yeast
> 2¾ cups (14 ounces) unbleached all-purpose flour

The dough
> ¾ cup (6 ounces) cold tap water
> 1¼ teaspoons active dry yeast
> 1½ cups (7½ ounces) unbleached all-purpose flour
> 1½ cups (9 ounces) coarse whole wheat flour
> 1 tablespoon salt

Make the starter

Pour the water into a medium bowl. Sprinkle the yeast over it and wait until it becomes creamy, about 5 minutes. Add the flour and mix vigorously with a rubber spatula. Cover the bowl with plastic wrap and leave it at room temperature (75°F) for 3 hours. It will double, and the entire surface will be bubbly.

Make the dough

Pour the water into the bowl of a heavy-duty mixer. Sprinkle the yeast over it and wait until it dissolves. Scrape the starter into the bowl, then add the flours and salt. Use the dough hook to mix everything together, then knead the dough on medium speed for 10 minutes. Cover the bowl with plastic wrap and let the dough rise at room temperature until it doubles in bulk, about 2 hours.

Shape the bread

Turn the dough onto a lightly floured surface and divide it into halves. Shape each piece into a ball. Line 2 small bowls with floured kitchen towels. Put the rounds into the bowls upside down, sprinkle them with flour, and fold the ends of the towels over them. Place the bowls in a large plastic bag and leave them at room temperature until the rounds double in size, about 1½ hours.

Bake the bread

Place a large, empty baking pan at the lowest level of the oven.

Preheat the oven to 450°F for 45 minutes with baking stones on the middle rack.

When the dough is ready, bring 2 cups water to a boil.

Remove the bowls from the plastic bag. Turn the dough out onto a floured peel and make decorative cuts in the top of each round with a single-edge razor. Slide the rounds onto the baking stones with a flick of the wrist. Immediately pour the water into the baking pan. *Caution*: This will cause an immediate burst of steam. Wear oven mitts and stand back to avoid being burned. Don't open the oven door for the first 10 minutes, or the steam will escape.

Bake the bread until it is well browned and sounds hollow when thumped on the bottom, 30 to 35 minutes. Cool on a rack.

BIBLIOGRAPHY

Arora, David. *All That the Rain Promises, and More*. Berkeley: Ten Speed Press, 1991.

Ashworth, Suzanne. *Seed to Seed*. Decorah, Iowa: Seed Saver Publications, 1991.

Auzet, Roger, Jean-Yves Guinard, and Pierre Lesjean. *L'Équipe de France de Boulangerie*. Les Lilas, France: Éditions Jérôme Villette, 1994.

Barberousse, Michel. *Cuisine Normande*. Paris: Éditions Barberousse, n.d. (author collection).

Blanc, Georges. *Ma Cuisine des Saisons*. Paris: Robert Laffont, 1984.

Blanchon, H. *Culture des Champignons et de la Truffe*. Paris: J. Rousset, 1906.

Boily, Lise, and Jean-François Blanchette. *The Bread Ovens of Quebec*. Seattle: University of Washington Press, 1979.

Cook, L. Russell. *Chocolate Production and Use*. Revised by Dr. E. H. Meursing. New York: Harcourt Brace Jovanovich, 1982.

Cronin, Isaac, Jay Harlow, and Paul Johnson. *The California Seafood Cookbook*. Berkeley: Aris Books, 1983.

Czarnecki, Jack. *A Cook's Book of Mushrooms*. New York: Artisan, 1995.

Dahl, Roald. *Charlie and the Chocolate Factory*. New York: Knopf, 1964.

Danell, Eric, and Francisco J. Camacho. "Successful Cultivation of the Golden Chanterelle." *Nature*, January 23, 1997, 303.

David, Elizabeth. *English Bread and Yeast Cookery*. Albuquerque: National Book Network, 1995.

Edwards, John. *The Roman Cookery of Apicius*. Point Roberts, Wash.: Hartley & Marks, 1984.

Ferguson, Louise, G. Steven Sibbett, and George C. Martin. *Olive Production Manual*. Publication 3353. Oakland: University of California, 1994.

Garro, Angelo. "Home-Cured Olives." *Fine Cooking*, December 1995/January 1996, 65-67.

Grigson, Jane. *The Mushroom Feast*. New York: Lyons and Burford, 1975.

———. *Jane Grigson's Vegetable Book*. New York: Atheneum, 1979.

———. *Jane Grigson's Fruit Book*. New York: Atheneum, 1982.

Guérard, Michel. *La Cusine Gourmande*. Paris: Éditions Robert Laffont, 1978.

Hess, Karen, transcriber. *Martha Washington's Booke of Cookery*. New York: Columbia University Press, 1995.

Hinault, Francis, and Joseph Koscher. *Les Recettes de la Table Bretonne*. Paris: Éditions Casteilla, 1957.

Howard, Robert, and Eric Skjei. *What Makes the Crops Rejoice*. Boston: Little, Brown, 1986.

Jacquemont, Guy, and Paul Mereaud. *Le Grand Livre du Beaujolais*. Malesherbes, France: Chêne, 1985.

Jenkins, Steven. *Cheese Primer*. New York: Workman Publishing, 1996.

Jordan, Michele Anna. *The Good Cook's Book of Tomatoes*. Menlo Park, Calif.: Addison-Wesley, 1995.

Kennedy, Diana. *The Art of Mexican Cooking*. New York: Bantam, 1989.

Klein, Maggie Blyth. *The Feast of the Olive*. Berkeley: Aris Books, 1983.

Kummer, Corby. "Where Chocolate Grows on Trees." *Atlantic Monthly*, October 1995, 110–113.

Lianides, Leon. "Quinces." *Gourmet*, October 1988, 90, 152–156.

Mariner, M. A. "A Lemon of Our Own." *San Francisco Chronicle*, February 21, 1996.

Martin, Alice A. *All About Apples*. Boston: Houghton Mifflin, 1976.

McClane, A. J. *The Encyclopedia of Fish Cookery*. New York: Holt, Rinehart & Winston, 1977.

McMahan, Jacqueline Higuera. *California Rancho Cooking*. Kingsport, Tenn.: The Olive Press, 1983.

———. "It Takes a Tamale to Truly Summon the Christmas Spirit." *San Francisco Chronicle*, December 10, 1997.

McPhee, John. *Oranges*. New York: Farrar, Straus & Giroux, 1967.

Michalak, Patricia S. *Rodale's Successful Organic Gardening Vegetables*. Emmaus, Pa.: Rodale Press, 1993.

Miller, Mark, Stephan Pyles, and John Sedlar. *Tamales*. New York: Macmillan, 1997.

Montagné, Prosper. *Nouveau Larousse Gastronomique*. Paris: Librairie Larousse, 1967.

Oster, Maggie. *The Potato Garden*. New York: Harmony Books, 1993.

Pourrat, Henri. *The Roquefort Adventure*. Trans. by Mary Mian. Société Anonyme des Caves et des Producteurs Rénuis de Roquefort, Roquefort-sur-Soulzon, 1956.

Ray, Richard, and Lance Walheim. *Citrus*. Los Angeles: Horticultural Publishing, 1980.

Raphael, Ray. *An Everyday History of Somewhere*. New York: Knopf, 1974.

Rigdon, Joan E. "Californians Claim to Unearth Secret of Raising Truffles." *Wall Street Journal*, March 25, 1994.

Robertson, Laurel. *The Laurel's Kitchen Bread Book*. New York: Random House, 1984.

Robinson, Jancis, ed. *The Oxford Companion to Wine*. Oxford: Oxford University Press, 1994.

Ronniger's Seed & Potato Co. catalog. Ellensburg, Wash., 1998.

Root, Waverley. *Food*. New York: Simon & Schuster, 1980.

Schaechter, Elio. *In the Company of Mushrooms*. Cambridge: Harvard University Press, 1997.

Schneider, Elizabeth. *Uncommon Fruits and Vegetables*. New York: Harper & Row, 1986.

———. "Where the Chocolate Tree Blooms." *Saveur*, September/October 1995, 96–106.

Sibbett, G. Steven, and Joseph Connell. *Producing Olive Oil in California*. Publication 21516. Oakland: University of California, 1994.

Sokolov, Raymond. "Quince Essentials." *Natural History*, August 1982: 78–80.

———. *With the Grain*. New York: Knopf, 1996.

Sonoma Antique Apple Nursery catalog. Healdsburg, Calif., 1998

Tannahill, Reay. *Food in History*. New York: Stein and Day, 1973.

The Dirtman Journal: Messages from the Garden. Number 1. Covelo, Calif.: Yolla Bolly Press, 1976.

Thompson, Sylvia. *The Kitchen Garden*. New York: Bantam, 1995.

Troisgros, Jean, and Pierre Troisgros. *Cuisiniers à Roanne*. Paris: Éditions Robert Laffont, 1977.

Turgeon, Charlotte, "The Staff of Life." *Saturday Evening Post*, January/February 1979, 108–110.

Vaughn, Reese. *Home Pickling of Olives*. Publication 2758. Berkeley: University of California, 1980.

Vilmorin-Andrieux, M. M. *The Vegetable Garden*. London: John Murray, 1885.

INDEX

A

Appetizers
    Bruschetta with Anchovies, 119
    Mushroom Appetizer Puffs, 75–76
    Scandinavian Marinated Crayfish
        with Dill, 58–59
Apple dishes
    Apple Tart with Almond Cream,
        138–40
    Apples Baked in Pastry, 142–43
    Fresh Apple Salsa, 141
    Quince and Apple Pinwheel
        Galettes, 112–13
    Warm Cabbage Salad with Apples,
        144–145
Apple Farm, Anderson Valley, 133–36,
    141
Apple Tart with Almond Cream,
    138–40
Apples
    cutting method, 135
    flavor, varieties, cooking qualities,
        133–37
    tree varieties, resources, 133–37
Apples Baked in Pastry, 142–43
Artisan bread, xvii–xviii
    Bay Area history, 205–10

B

Bakeries
    Citizen Cake, 15–17, 18, 24
    Downtown Bakery and Creamery,
        Healdsburg, 20, 22, 125
    Fran Gage Pâtisserie Française, xvii,
        11–15, 61–64, 134–35, 205–06

Bakers' Dozen, 13
Balboa Cafe, 41, 42
Bates, Karen & Tim, 133–36, 141
Beaujolais Nouveau
    food accompaniments, 148–49,
        150, 151–52
    parties in San Francisco, 147–48
Belgian food, xx–xxi, 40, 44, 51, 53
Bellwether Farms (cheese), 171–74,
    178, 180
Bernachon chocolates, 27–28
Bertolli, Paul, 2
Blanc, Georges, 56
Blood oranges
    Blood Orange Mousse Cake,
        166–68
    Citrus Salad with Fennel, 169
    varieties, 161–63
Books on food and cooking, 219–21
Boonville Farmers' Market, 2, 136
Boyd, Rod, 144
Bread and baking
    Alan Scott and Ovencrafters, 14,
        206–10
    Bay Area history, xvii–xviii, 205–10
    Bay Village Wood Fire Baking
        (bread), 209–10, 214
    flour sources, 211
    pain au levain starter, 205
    rye bread, sponge starters, 192–93,
        211–13
    sourdough yeast organisms, 208
    whole wheat bread starter, 216–17

The author and her red 1967 Alfa Romeo

About the Author

Fran Gage owned and operated the highly respected Fran Gage Pâtisserie Française for ten years, until it was closed following a fire in 1995. The bakery attained critical acclaim locally and nationally for its pastries, breads, and chocolates. Ms. Gage taught pastry and bread-making classes at the bakery and throughout California. She is largely a self-taught cook, but she has had formal training at the original La Varenne in Paris, and at Ecole Lenôtre. She now devotes her time to teaching and writing, with articles appearing in *Fine Cooking, Kitchen Gardener*, and *Saveur*. She lives with her husband in San Francisco.